Toward Mastery

A Smith and Kraus Book
Published by Smith and Kraus, Inc.
PO Box 127, Lyme, NH 03768

Copyright © 1998 by Jean Hackett
All rights reserved
Manufactured in the United States of America

First Edition: December 1998
10 9 8 7 6 5 4 3 2 1

CAUTION: Professionals and amateurs are hereby warned that the material represented in this book is fully protected under the copyright laws of the United States of America, and of all countries covered by the International Copyright Union (including the Dominion of Canada and the rest of the British Commonwealth), and of all countries covered by the Pan-American Copyright Convention and the Universal Copyright Convention, and of all countries with which the United States has reciprocal copyright relations. All rights, including professional, amateur, motion picture, recitation, lecturing, public reading, radio broadcasting, television, video or sound taping, all other forms of mechanical or electronic reproductions such as CD-ROM and CD-I, information storage and retrieval systems and photocopying, and the rights of translation into foreign languages, are strictly reserved. Particular emphasis is laid upon the question of public readings, permission for which must be secured from Smith and Kraus, Inc.

Cover and text design by Julia Hill Gignoux, Feedom Hill Design
Cover photo used with kind permission of Williamstown Theater Festival

Library of Congress Cataloging-in-Publication Data

Psacharopoulos, Nikos, d.1989.
Toward mastery: Nikos Psacharopoulos in the classroom /
edited by Jean Hackett with Gregory Boyd... [et al.]. —1st ed.
p. cm. — (Career development series)
ISBN 1-57525-166-3
1. Psacharopoulos, Nikos, d.1989. 2. Acting.
I. Hackett, Jean. II. Title. III. Series.
PN2061.P74   1998
792'.028—dc21   98-36283
CIP

Toward Mastery
An Acting Class
with Nikos Psacharopoulos

edited by Jean Hackett

with commentary by
*Gregory Boyd, Steve Lawson, Lynne Meadow,
Bonnie Monte, Tom Moore, Austin Pendleton,
David Schweizer, and Joanne Woodward*

CAREER DEVELOPMENT SERIES

A Smith and Kraus Book

...It is our task to find out first if they have talent, second to expose them to different methods of working, and finally, to have them discover and cultivate their own individual approach and style. What we really want for them is, to quote Peer Gynt, "to be yourself," which is "to kill the worst and so bring out the best in yourself."

Nikos Psacharopoulos
from a letter to Robert Brustein
regarding the Yale School of Drama
February 24, 1967

Contents

Foreword
    THE SEA OF NPs: Steve Lawson VII

Introduction
    AN ACTOR'S JOURNEY: Jean Hackett XIII

Part One: Beginnings: Bad Acting
    ACTING ONE 1
    THINKING VS. ACTING *(A Streetcar Named Desire)* 6
    BANISHING THEATRICALITY 10
    BOTCHED EXPERIMENTS *(The Glass Menagerie)* 16
    SUGAR-COATING *(The Killing of Sister George)* 20
    COMMENTARY: Joanne Woodward 29

Part Two: Pitfalls
    LANGUAGE TRAPS *(In the Jungle of Cities)* 34
    CHARACTER CRUTCHES 39
    SEXUALITY AND DANGER *(Miss Julie)* 44
    OBVIOUS CHOICES *(Les Liaisons Dangereuses)* 47
    PREMEDITATED ACTING *(Uncle Vanya)* 53
    COMMENTARY: Lynne Meadow 59

Part Three: "Drop By Drop, Knowledge Comes to the Unwilling"
    ACTING WITHOUT PURPOSE *(Golden Boy)*............63
    AGAINST INTERPRETATION *(In the Boom Boom Room)*....68
    TOUCHING BASE *(Ivanov)* 76
    MALADJUSTED ACTING *(A Taste of Honey)*............80
    TO KNOW AND NOT TO KNOW *(The Runner Stumbles)* ...85
    COMMENTARY: David Schweizer....................90

Part Four: Breakthroughs
    LETTING GO *(Cat on a Hot Tin Roof)* 95
    ACTING WITHOUT IMPOSITION *(True West)* 102
    ACTING IN EXCESS *(Benefactors)* 105
    MESSING IT UP *(Uncle Vanya)*.......................111
    COMMENTARY: Bonnie Monte 117

Part Five: Artistic License
    PROMISE *(Julia)*..................................121
    PHYSICAL COMEDY *(Private Lives)*..................124
    WORDS AND DEEDS *(Les Liaisons Dangereuses)*..........127
    POINT OF VIEW *(A Streetcar Named Desire)*.............133
    COMMENTARY: Gregory Boyd 137

Part Six: Toward Mastery
    SHARPENING TECHNIQUE *(Betrayal)* 140
    TELLING THE STORY 142
    MAKING SKETCHES *(Ashes)*.......................147
    PLAYING WITH SHAW *(Mrs. Warren's Profession)* 155
    PUTTING IT TOGETHER *(Uncle Vanya)*...............162
    COMMENTARY: Austin Pendleton..................182

Afterword
    COME TO THE EDGE: Tom Moore 186

Foreword
The Sea of NPs

BY STEVE LAWSON

I knew Nikos Psacharopoulos for twenty years, but never studied with him. Not formally. But because his classroom style dovetailed closely with his director's persona, in all the roles I played for Nikos — p.r. and box office gofer, sound techie, personal assistant (a job akin to trench warfare), actor, literary manager, director, playwright — I never stopped learning.

    Stanley Kauffmann once asked his film students to describe what they knew about Charlie Chaplin, and one wrote that he wasn't sure but thought that Chaplin knew a great deal about him. That sounds like Nikos and many of us: While few ever plumbed the Sea of NPs to its unsounded depths, he always knew a hell of a lot about how *you* operated. Take the purely mercenary level. He had an uncanny nose for anticipating the moment when I'd rebel at my paltry Williamstown Theater Festival (WTF) salary and demand a stunning $5-a-week raise. Out of the blue, Nikos would collar me in the hall and whisper conspiratorially in that semi-fathomable accent: "Aaaah, yah — you know, Stephen — I think maybe it's time you were, like, kind of — an Associate Director. Ahkay?" Bowled over by the unexpected honor, I'd forget all about the raise…his strategy all along. *Let them eat titles!*

Among the many Nikosian gems in this book, two stick out because they applied to me as a twenty- or thirty-something: "You're doodling rather than painting" and "When you are fairly young, you try to clutter everything." I stayed young for a long time; I shed my clutter reluctantly. But with Nikos hovering implacably as a kind of *uber*-shit detector, I simplified. A turning point came when WTF's experimental company mounted a season of new American plays, and I directed David Mamet's little-known *Squirrels;* the three actors and I struggled and sweated to do this difficult piece justice. After opening night, Nikos beckoned me over, looking grim. (My heart sank.) "You know —" he began, and frowned. (My heart stopped sinking and just stopped.) Then a crooked smile tugged at his mouth. "You know — nobody could have gotten more out of it than you did." And he vanished into the night. I'm not sure Mamet would've appreciated the sentiment, but at the time I felt that I'd been tapped on the shoulder with a sword.

But with Nikos, there was no resting on laurels. He panned my next effort, grousing I hadn't had fun with it, had settled for a tame production. "If you're going to fail," he cried, "do it in a big way!" Whoa! Enough to make me yearn for another week of rehearsal, so we could come up with a truly *majestic* flop.

Though I wasn't a student per se, with any real proximity to Nikos the education was full tilt and ongoing. But you'll learn from these pages even if you never met the man. And if you haven't yet read the previous book Jean Hackett published (Smith and Kraus, 1994), put that one on your shelf, too. *The Actor's Chekhov*, a fascinating collage of interviews with performers about their work on twenty-five years of Chekhov productions at Williamstown, is the mirror image of *Toward*

Mastery. The first book is public-oriented, with gifted artists musing on a single genius in terms of performance. This new volume is its private bookend, and the stress is on the classroom: Nikos as a Prospero to aspiring Mirandas and Ferdinands. In *The Actor's Chekhov*, the focus is on leading actors with success under their belts; in *Toward Mastery*, the next generation occupies center stage.

Toward Mastery has several virtues. First, it takes you right into the kitchen, plunging into the crazy, tangled, often maddening process outlined in Hackett's introduction. ("Nikos invariably strove for chaos.") His classes were anything but linear roads on the way to enlightenment — here are unexpected detours, dead-ends when all seems lost, exhilarating freeways when inspiration strikes and the work takes off like a Porsche.

Once you put this book down, you'll have crossed an ocean of vivid detail: what Nikos knows about playwrights in relation to students, or why he likes to rehearse *The Three Sisters* out of order. How major talents such as Blythe Danner or Olympia Dukakis can light up an audition room, or why the personal techniques Joanne Woodward or Meryl Streep or Christopher Walken use may work for them but not others. Why intellect and instinct are different fish. How even a harsh remark is designed to guide neophyte actors into a fresh take on the material. (Most irresistible of the latter is the critique of a wrong-headed interpretation of Strindberg's erotic *Miss Julie:* Nikos suggests that when this Jean and Julie exit they aren't going to have sex but to play with balloons.)

Second, the book tells you a great deal you didn't know. Not merely the anecdotes, which I could linger on for a long time…especially the story about the female cabbie who regales Nikos with violent feelings toward Lee Strasberg though Nikos keeps telling her that he's dead. On a serious level, the in-depth analyses are worth any actor's time: The scale of emotional bells Anya can ring when she sees the nursery in *The Cherry Orchard,* or how the titanic first act between Brick and Maggie in *Cat on a Hot Tin Roof* should go (in four lightning pages here, one of the finest exegeses of a play in my experience).

Even passing comments illuminate, because they raise large issues. In drama school, critic Richard Gilman once asked if we really wanted to meet Raskolnikov or the Karamazovs in a dark alley; similarly, Nikos makes the startling statement here that "you can't have theater with normal people." (If art were like life, who would need it?) Then, like an arrow, he hones in on the specific to clinch his argument:

> *If Blanche in* Streetcar *says, "Well, I'm sorry, I'll stay out of your way, Stanley, I will not drink, I'll keep my hands off boys, and I'll go back to my little room," she'd be okay. She'd get her pension and there wouldn't be a play.*

Third — the litmus test of any book — you're left wanting more. This is partly inadvertent: While distilling the class tapes into transcripts, Hackett was stymied because certain scenes went verbally unidentified. We managed to figure out a few on the basis of character names or references, but several still remain tantalizingly out of reach. Still, isn't that part of making art? You *can't* know everything all the time in the theater: Truth comes at you in shards and fragments. Which is why the directors' comments after each section and Tom Moore's afterword are so provocative and deeply felt: Each person gives his or her perspective on Nikos from a uniquely shared experience, an individual twist of the kaleidescope.

Short of the sadly impossible, hearing his actual voice again — that Greek diction refreshed annually by a pilgrimage back to his beloved isle of Siphnos; the rapid-fire, anserine delivery culminating in a long "Aaaaahhh!" (cue to laugh) — *Toward Mastery* gives us Nikos again in all his complexity: kind/cruel, hilarious/somber, candid/elusive. Paradox could've been his middle name: The more he thought of your talent and potential — and you see this in the arc of the book, from the stumblers all the way up to those on the brink of full professionalism — the more demanding he could be.

Vicarious trip: We watch these hopeful kids taking their first tentative steps, only to be rapped on the knuckles by Nikos ("Don't be so eager to act"). Advancing a little, only to fall back ("Throw it all away…You just seem to be a happy doormat!"). Then, gingerly moving ahead again, hearing some slightly left-handed praise ("Your best moment was when the prop didn't work for you…wonderful!"). Finally, reward in the shape of outright endorsement ("The kind of work we want — that is what, at the end of the day, really counts for a lot. Good life, wonderful acting.") How appropriate, the final sentence out of his mouth: "Getting there is *all* the fun." A dizzying roller coaster of a man and a book…and we're along for the ride.

When I think of Nikos — few days go by when I don't — I often flash back to a stanza from "Little Gidding." Four lines which somehow embody this mentor, my own and that of many others:

> *We shall not cease from exploration*
> *And the end of all our exploring*
> *Will be to arrive where we started*
> *And know the place for the first time.*

To an intrepid explorer like Nikos, the unceasing process, the drive to know, was the thing that made him happiest. He was a life-affirming Ahab fording a tempestuous sea, fiercely on the lookout to reel in any and all nuances of the actor's art. So I'm grateful this book exists. *Toward Mastery* documents — in print, and for as long as anyone cares about excellence in the theater — just what gave Nikos Psacharopoulos his greatest joy.

Associated with Williamstown Theater Festival since age nineteen, Steve Lawson was its first dramaturg, has adapted ten novels for its stages, and created a new translation of La Ronde *for a production directed by Joanne Woodward. He has received a Christopher Award and Emmy and Humanitas nominations for such television credits as* The Elephant Man, The Room Upstairs, St. Elsewhere, Jonathan, *and* Broadway's Dreamers: The Legacy of the Group Theatre.

Introduction
An Actor's Journey
by Jean Hackett

But for his untimely death a decade ago, January 1999 would have been the occasion of Nikos Psacharopoulos' seventieth birthday. The renowned Williamstown Theatre Festival, which he helped found in 1955 and where he served as Artistic/Executive Director for thirty-three years, continues to grow and flourish as an artistic haven for actors — celebrated ones as well as new, undiscovered, talent. But Nikos' legacy does not just reside at WTF — it lives on vibrantly in the thousands of young people he trained and guided over the thirty-five years of his teaching career. Many of his former students, apprentices and interns have become well-known actors, many are or have been artistic directors of major American regional theaters, as well as television and film directors, playwrights and screenwriters, composers, designers, stage managers, arts administrators, producers, agents, and casting directors. An extraordinary number of people across the country cut their creative teeth on Nikos' aesthetic and work ethic and carry his vision with them like a banner into their fields of expertise.

Three years before his death in 1989, Nikos and I began audio-taping his class sessions in preparation for a book on acting. In 1994, slightly sidetracked, I finished writing and editing *The Actor's Chekhov*, a compilation of interviews and acting lessons based on Nikos' extensive lifework on the plays of Anton Chekhov at Williamstown. *Toward Mastery* is the book we'd always intended to do — a series of acting lessons drawn from critiques of scene work that attempts to give, in overview and specifics, the essential elements that Nikos believed made for great acting.

SETTING THE STAGE:
THE CLASS ENVIRONMENT

Most of this century's great acting teachers' careers flourished after their professional careers had waned. Throughout Nikos' life, however, his active career as a director fed and enhanced his equally consuming career as a teacher. His classes existed not in the abstract but the concrete: For Nikos, his student's scene work provided an experimental canvas for work he had just finished or was preparing to do. And for his students, the atmosphere was rife with possibility, as Nikos often plucked actors from his classroom talent pool to join the acting company in Williamstown.

Nikos began his teaching career at Yale, his grad school alma mater, in 1954, the year before he became one of the founders of WTF. He continued to teach at Yale at least one day a week for the rest of his life and also taught at Amherst, Williams, Columbia, N.Y.U., and Circle in the Square. In 1975, he formed a private class for professional actors that he ran for almost fifteen years. His Manhattan classes were conducted in spaces all over the city — at Circle in the Square, in the rehearsal room over the old Circle Downtown, in the ballroom of the now defunct Martinique Hotel on

33rd Street, and in various theaters and rehearsal rooms on 42nd Street's Theater Row. But the structure of his two-hour class sessions never varied: Students presented three scenes per class (hopefully none longer than ten minutes) for Nikos' evaluation and critique.

Studying with Nikos could best be described as intensely terrifying fun, with each session suffused with an aura of import. These two hours were not casual. Nikos made clear from the beginning, not in words but in his attitude toward the sessions, that every minute of the time demanded complete focus and concentration, that no one would come late or leave early, and above all that no one would ever disturb scene work in progress. Students were expected to arrive fully prepared with lines memorized, appropriate props, and even set pieces and costumes. Given all this, Nikos never played the disciplinarian. The structure he imposed was not about "rules," but about creating an environment where the work took precedence over everything else. Within these tight parameters, Nikos let loose the possibility of a creative free-for-all — encouraging students to go full-out in their emotional, vocal, and physical commitment to the scene, to leap at any and all opportunities for making fools of themselves. As he was fond of saying: "If you're going to fail, fail trying to be successful. Don't fail because you're too *scared* to be successful."

Even when teaching first-year classes, Nikos began at a more advanced level than most acting teachers. He never turned a class session into an acting homework session (as so many acting teachers tend to do), taking for granted that his students were already well-versed and adept at developing the character's back-story, working with objectives and obstacles, sense and emotional memory, imagination, and so forth. Nor did he delve into aspects of the actor's private life and assume the role of psychoanalyst rather than teacher. He would, sometimes, offer actors personal insights about themselves. I once heard him say to a young actress, "You know the work is wonderful, except why is that vibrato constantly in your voice? We get it that you are emotional, stop playing your own violins!" But for Nikos, actively sifting through or seeking to expose the actor's private emotional source material was anathema.

Nikos was also less interested in the actor's interpretations or "choices" in a scene than he was in how the actor executed these choices. Speaking of students auditioning for his professional class in a 1985 interview, he said:

> *For a class I like to see somebody who is 'working,' who's making the audition a process rather than a result. That shows me what the person is rather than what they do. It's just like doing scales — emotional scales — the way a singer would come and sing a few notes. I don't really worry about the melody, I don't really worry about the interpretation of the play... Unfortunately, too many times directors love to have choices made by actors, because then they don't have to make choices. I basically believe I can make any choice I want to for an actor; I just want actors to do them well.*

Even as a director Nikos was mistrustful and disinterested in talking about "interpretation." As Austin Pendleton says in his interview in *The Actor's Chekhov*: "Nikos, like a lot of master directors or conductors, wasn't into intellectual debate about the play. Nikos knew what he *felt* the play was about and he encouraged you to live in his feeling about the play. And his feelings…always came from an authentic place in him, they had an organic logic."

He was nothing if not a purist. In running a theater company, he was sometimes forced against his better judgement to make compromises, which he sometimes got away with and sometimes paid for. But in the classroom, that pure arena, only the "work" existed, unfettered by exigencies of politics, grants, or ticket sales. Yet for Nikos, even that pure arena was not a vacuum: In his mind scene work always existed in direct relationship to an opening night. In the classroom he operated very much as he did in the rehearsal room: as if imminently the work would be presented to the world, and the urgency of his comments and exhortations reflects this. Time was at a premium for Nikos, and in class he invariably seemed to be racing against it — as if on the one hand, to protect his students' talent from a raging epidemic of mediocrity (and bad directors), and on the other to save the world of plays he loved from actors' misguided machinations. As a result, student actors in his classes were called to standards no different than professionals in the midst of preparing for the most important work of their lives.

When scenes were presented, Nikos could often be more watchable than the work on stage. He never "sat back" or held himself at a distance — he participated in the subtext and emotion of the scene with his whole being. If the work really took a course down the wrong road, he became restless, in frustration running a hand through his hair over and over, and then (usually after only four or five lines) jumping up and interrupting the scene, calling out: "Okay, I have to stop it!" — almost as if allowing the scene to continue would seriously endanger everyone in the room. From there, with a rushing onslaught of words he would attempt to get this emergency of bad acting under control, finally giving the actors direction and allowing the scene to start again.

But most often he let the scene play out, watching from the edge of his seat, his face mirroring the intensity of the work, his inner being riding along in the same roller-coaster seat as the actors onstage, sharing with them the bumpy moment-by-moment ride through the emotional terrain of the play. In the critique afterwards, he did not "chat." His vocal energy reflected the same high-stakes realm of the characters in the play; he relived the scene in critique with the same muscularity, tension, and conviction he saw — or wanted to see. His heightened involvement penetrated the work in a visceral way, and his critique expressed not just his ideas about the scene but a precise translation of the actors' experience while playing it. His uncanny ability to articulate the inarticulate of the actor's process was to a great extent communicated by his tone of voice, his inflections, his physical energy. As much as possible in the acting lessons here, I have tried to indicate those. Nevertheless, it is almost impossible to convey on a page the visuals of Nikos' teaching: the body movements, gestures, the acting out of moments that transmitted his ideas sheerly on the gut level. Teaching for Nikos was never "talking," it was a two-hour marathon of emotion, ideas, and associations, from which both he and his students emerged exhilarated and breathing hard.

First-year actors now and then were given creative exercises — a day where we'd all come dressed as our favorite character, or an assignment to make a "character collage" from magazine pictures. When all else failed, Nikos could resort to getting physical with actors — having them play scenes with hand tied hands behind their backs, or while being restrained or poked or tickled by other actors — depending on what he was going for. Sometimes when a scene ended — no doubt beyond hope — Nikos would sit silent for a few moments and then say to one of the actors in the scene: "Okay, just — jump. Just keep jumping." (Or dance, or run around the stage.) "*Now* start the lines." This, usually, would throw the actor off. "You see!" he would yell triumphantly, "You cannot jump and talk at the same time!" It took us a while to learn that Nikos' goal was not some strange combo of physical and verbal dexterity, but to stop the actor from "thinking" about how to say the lines. The physical exertion he imposed enabled the lines to come out accidently, inevitably, in an unpremeditated way. Both as a director and a teacher, Nikos invariably strove for chaos: shaking up and pulling apart work that was composed, measured, choreographed or preconceived. His goal, always, was to "mess it up" — vocally, physically, and emotionally.

Applause after scene work was nixed — Nikos admonished early on that these were rehearsals, not performances. If he hadn't already stopped it or reworked it, at the end of a scene presentation Nikos would then turn to the class and abruptly say: "Yeah?" Which meant he was asking for comments on the work. (The actors in the actual scene did not speak — Nikos felt the work should speak for itself.) For first-year students, making comments on their fellow actors' work was a rather terrifying event, as Nikos critiqued not only the actors but the observers of acting, training students how to "see" what was happening on stage as much as to act. He would challenge comments that he felt were off-base by asking for a vote of how many others in the class saw the same thing. He rejected and cut off all comments that he called "interpretive" — nipping in the bud anything that started out with, "I think this character should played as…" or "This scene should be about…" He advised students over and over that as far as he was concerned there were no prototypes for anything, his exhortation something like — "Please don't tell me how you would like to see it or what your interpretation is, just speak about what you *saw*." His constant reality testing regarding text and behavior cultivated the actor's knack for recognizing and synthesizing nuanced meanings not just on stage but in everyday life.

Except to shut down interpretive comments, Nikos remained completely neutral toward students' remarks, neither agreeing or disagreeing with any of the comments: His mind about the scene had long since been made up and the class responses served merely as a forum for him to learn more about each individual student's thought process. Sometimes he reworked a scene before critiquing it by going up onstage and whispering a few seconds of direction to each actor. Usually the second time through the work changed radically, and students then were expected to make distinctions between what they saw in each version of the scene. Although the students' remarks for the most part went unacknowledged, occasionally in the course of the critique itself, Nikos would validate something a student had said: "Well, David was on target when he told you —" or "Christina said something very interesting about —." As Nikos never bothered with small talk before or after class, and was virtually unapproachable outside of the classroom, students were often shocked or thrilled to realize that Nikos not only knew their names but remembered specific comments they had made weeks before. He would not hesitate, after hearing a slew of positive comments to say something like, "Well, I'm glad they all like you, because I hated it." (Or the opposite.)

When Nikos was on a roll, his quick intelligence, humor, and inimitable style were mesmerizing. As I wrote in my introduction to *The Actor's Chekhov*, it is impossible to capture on the page the rapid, Greek-accented speech or his propensity for putting words together in patterns different from anything you heard before or ever would again. Often Nikos' own personal brand of the English language came out in ways that were funny. (Giving a direction to two groups of actors on opposite sides of a stage in a crowd scene: "All right everybody, when I say go, you CRISS, and you CROSS!") But most often, Nikos' rather original use of the language allowed the listener to hear, and perhaps perceive in new ways too. Oblique and enigmatic outside of the classroom, as a teacher and director he was crystal clear about his feelings, even if it took some time to get used to his verbal shorthand and incredibly quick, accented speech.

Nikos often got angry if a scene was bad, angrier still if he believed in the talent of the actors involved, and most infuriated of all if the actors had imposed a bogus interpretation on plays he held dear. A frequent exasperated comment: "Chekhov's / Shakespeare's / Brecht's ideas are much more interesting than yours will ever be, so why don't you just do what's there!" As a rule of thumb, the more he believed in a student's work the more likely he was to get agitated — but it was a positive anger, rather like his exhortations to actors in confrontation scenes to fight "for" rather than "against" something. Never mincing words, Nikos could be cutting, sarcastic, acerbic, even devastating, but still you had the sense that he was fighting for your work to succeed. When a scene went wrong, especially with actors whose work he liked, the tirade that spewed forth went something like: "How could you do this to yourselves? What were you thinking? And how is it that I had to watch you mangle this great material?" And it *was* always great material: Nikos approved in advance which plays actors could work on, and if a student suggested a scene from a play Nikos considered inferior, he would say, "Well, you can do it if you want, but I won't be able to help you with it, because that play just is, you know, *bad!*"

The class was not for everyone. Nikos often had a deep antagonism, both when he directed and taught, toward actors he perceived as impenetrable — whose facade or defenses did not allow for "messiness" and the emotional transparency he believed vital for exciting work. He had big problems working with students he judged as "not bright," as well as with those who actively fought him. He had absolutely no time for actors who disagreed with him or challenged his point of view. A student who did not like his diagnosis ought to go elsewhere for a second opinion, not argue with him about it. It was not about ego, but about time, and he had none to waste explaining his thoughts, as he frequently said, "ad nauseam."

And indeed, as an acting teacher Nikos considered himself more a diagnostician than a philosopher. In a way, Nikos believed there were as many different acting techniques as there were actors, and absolutely nothing applied to everyone. In a 1987 interview he said: "This constant need to define the art world with words is very problematic. I never know what people mean. I only know what I see and what I hear. And that's why I think you can't really write a textbook about acting. The easiest way of showing something about acting is to use a videotape. With a tape you see what is really happening." But despite his reluctance to be pinned down, Nikos did, slowly but surely, impart to students who studied with him over a period of years a set of highly specific skills and values.

Most concretely, his technique consisted of an array of tools for approaching various playwrights. His knowledge of text was formidable, and with the trial and error of years of experience, he had codified for himself certain well-defined "absolutes" for highly differentiated approaches to plays by all the great writers and most of the semi-greats. Some of the technical gems in my own class notes include things like: "The humor in Coward doesn't come from the way the voice colors the words, it comes from a split-second pause taken before certain well-chosen words." Or: "In a Shakespeare comedy when you're given a letter to read, never deal with 'I'm puzzled.' Deal with the fun of it, read it as if you know exactly what it's about and let the question come in afterward." Or: "When Williams gives you a speech, always play that you'll never get to finish it, that you have so many more words pent up inside you that you'll never get to say." Or: "Shaw has to be done with much more emotion than Chekhov or Williams because of the length of the lines. Shaw's characters are just as passionate as anyone else's — except they are passionate about ideas, not feelings." Or, on Molière: "The effort to keep the mask in place, the fight to keep the mask in place is what gives the style. Style is not a result of the period, or the language, but the strength of the obstacle." These gems and countless others we scribbled in our notebooks and built our technique on were invaluable.

But the heart of his teaching was that which is often considered the most sophisticated and most innate component of talent: taste. Through years of observation, insight, and application he had formulated for himself a material set of processes and values that he felt had to be present for great acting to occur. Nikos had no interest in "serviceable" or middle-of-the-road acting. He was only interested in what makes up *great* acting; the reason why some work is brilliant and some passes unnoticed; why certain actors' emotional worlds move us and others' leave us cold; why certain voices compel us to listen and others tune us out; why the inner life of one is mesmerizing in a moment of stillness and another's is boring in the midst of histrionics. Yet even when dealing with the metaphysics of acting, Nikos was the least metaphysical of teachers: He did not relegate these seemingly mystical qualities to the luck of the draw. For those who studied with him over a period of time, the answer to the eternal question "Can acting be taught?" was certain. Nikos' most profound gift was an ineluctable sureness that the aesthetic qualities that made for great work were at their core processes as teachable, as apprehensible, as usable as the most basic technical tools. If it was not given to everyone to achieve great acting, it was at least possible to know how to attempt it.

A favorite comment, a reward, from Nikos, came something like this: "You know, there were problems in the beginning and problems with your voice, and you have no idea how to use this language, but the moment when you let loose and fell down/looked at him/tore up that letter/walked to the door" (whatever) "was just — spine-chilling!" He would go on to illuminate what made that particular moment different, what accounted for the "spine-chilling" effect of it, but in achieving that moment and eventually others, the student actor developed the core of his aspiration and standards, and a clearly defined value system to strive for throughout his professional life. What constitutes great work is the running theme of *Toward Mastery*.

USING THE ACTING CRITIQUES

The critiques here are transcribed from sessions audiotaped between 1986 and 1988, taken from classes ranging from first-year to his advanced workshop for professional actors. Arranged in six sequential sections, the material attempts to mirror the journey many students experienced studying with Nikos over a period of years. Each of the six sections is followed by commentary from a director who either studied or worked with Nikos in the formative stages of his or her career, and each individual critique is prefaced by a note identifying the scene itself and the topics discussed. Unfortunately, Nikos and I were often haphazard in taping the sessions, in fact, it was not until two years after his death that I listened to all of the tapes in their entirety. Many times we forgot to record the titles of scenes being presented, and despite my best efforts and those of some of the smartest dramaturgs around, several of the scenes addressed here cannot be identified. When a scene defies identification, however, it is precisely because it serves merely as a blank slate for acting problems Nikos feels must be attended to before any specific work on the play itself can begin. As helpful as it always is to know which play is at issue, in most cases that information is not imperative for the reader to connect to what is being discussed.

In Part One, "Beginnings: Bad Acting," Nikos starts by stripping away the actor's clichéd and/or misguided ideas about acting and text interpretation; Part Two, "Pitfalls," defines traps the actor often falls into dealing with language, character, and behavior. Part Three, "Drop By Drop, Knowledge Comes to the Unwilling," encourages the actor's ability to access and use the circumstantial evidence in the text, and her growing trust in drawing on her own unique qualities rather than preconceived images. In Part Four, "Breakthroughs," the lessons center on, as Nikos puts it, "the real question…how well the actor has learned to give himself permission to use the acting equipment — his emotional world, his voice, his body and his attitude." Part Five, "Artistic License," speaks to originality in the work, the color and strength of the actor's inner landscape and verbal images, as well as directorial concepts such as point of view. Part Six, "Toward Mastery," explores a variety of issues surrounding virtuosity — realizing the specific demands of particular playwrights, merging craft and artistry, and fueling the internal and external conditions necessary to give rise to great acting.

Throughout, Nikos deals frequently with fundamentals, but not only fundamentals that the beginning actor must learn. The seasoned actor who has already built his acting vocabulary will hopefully find Nikos' way of delineating these fundamentals congruent with the more advanced task of paring down the work to its essential lines. Although the book moves "toward mastery," there is really no clear hierarchy in acting challenges: What is complex for some is simple for others and vice versa. Student actors, I hope, will find in *Toward Mastery* a reference to use over and over in each new phase of their development as artists. Seasoned actors will find Nikos' ideas and manner of presentation (even when dealing with the most basic acting problems) sophisticated, witty, and full of anecdote, and they hopefully will be able to use these critiques as a springboard for reconnecting to the enthusiasm of the beginning, a sort of "going home again" to the initial impulses that inspired the creative journey — and through those times, as Olympia Dukakis has said, where one's reasons for acting change and mature.

At issue for actors at every level of proficiency is Nikos' running theme: the question of what makes for great acting. I will not attempt, nor would I be able to reduce his formidable concepts to a few sentences, as the aesthetic and multilayered processes he offers cannot be absorbed in a purely linear or verbal way. It is the repetition, and the emphasis in that repetition of certain values revealing themselves in a myriad of scenarios, that builds to perception and understanding — which is why I use one of Nikos' favorite quotes ("Drop by drop, knowledge comes to the unwilling") as a title for the third section. Not only must new concepts be apprehended and incorporated in the actor's psyche, old ways of thinking and responding must be chipped away. This exists as process, as what some experts now call intrinsic or "fluid" learning (the "how") rather than the extrinsic or "crystallized" (the "what"). Nikos sums this up best in a 1986 interview when he says:

> *I think actors torture themselves too much by confusing acting and the acting instrument with decisions. I'm not saying people should not think, but I just believe that you often don't really know with a great painting or sculpture what the exact thought is, because the piece of art has to be stronger than the artist. Again, I'm not saying that actors should not think. All I'm saying is that if thought made us great artists, we'd all be Picassos. You've got to be able to play the instrument first, before you are an artist. If you play that instrument in a certain kind of way, then, of course, you become a dif-*

ferent kind of artist. But the point is, you can't just say that because you think, because your thoughts are great and your perception of the material is great, you're an artist. You're not. It is the emotional and the physical response that is important...Most of the people I work with are very bright. That's not what I'm talking about. I think acting is like the great Saint Joan *line: "I hear my voices first and I find reasons for them afterwards."*

The critiques can be read out of sequence, but I feel the actor will be best served by working straight through. I've tried to think of the whole as a piece of music, in which certain melody lines resonate more purely and definitively as the piece goes on — accentuated and revealed not just by tonal differences but in the use of rhythm and tempo as well. Along the way, riffs and digressions abound, but in the end, it is the cumulative effect of the composition that allows its power and meaning to unfold.

A PERSONAL JOURNEY

In 1976, as an undergraduate in the New York University (NYU) Drama Program, I was randomly placed in the Circle in the Square Theater School for my studio training. Thus began a chain of events that would shape my professional and personal life for years to come. I studied acting with Nikos for three years as an undergraduate and after graduation continued my training in his professional class. I was invited to become a member of the non-Equity acting company at the Williamstown Theatre Festival, where I returned over the years to work as a professional actress. Along the way, Nikos and I entered into a personal relationship and at the time of his death were engaged to be married. Now, living in Los Angeles almost ten years later, it is still impossible for me to attend any social event, theater production, or entertainment industry function without someone approaching me and saying something like "I just wanted to tell you, I was an apprentice / I was an assistant director / I studied with Nikos." This is usually followed by something to the effect of "and it changed my life."

My years at Circle/NYU were all a beginning should be — exhilarating, exhausting, inspirational, scary, wildly fun. Studio work at Circle included physical and vocal training, mime, training in the "Method," and scene study with a variety of teachers, the centerpiece for all involved being Nikos' class. After the first year, Nikos separated our class into two groups, and I was lucky enough to be chosen for the "A" group. There were about fourteen of us — most of whom are now working actors. For two years we worked together constantly, sometimes putting up three or four scenes a week. With all the manic energy and foolhardiness necessary for the start of the journey, we rehearsed into the wee hours night after night; competed, argued, directed each other, got drunk with each other, critiqued each other, watched each other grow. (In our third year together we developed with Nikos a project called "A Collage of Tennessee Williams" — a series of scenes and monologues in a thematic order that became the basis for the Williamstown Theater Festival's six-hour, two-part collage *Tennessee Williams: A Celebration*, for which Mr. Williams was in residence.) After the first two years, we got the feeling that Nikos actually liked our group a little bit more than some of the others (probably because we were so dogged in our efforts for his class) and eventually he invited most of us to join the non-Equity company at

Williamstown. There, we completed our immersion in his aesthetic in the true sense of the word "apprentice" — through hands-on, direct contact as we watched him work with some of America's greatest actors.

But probably it was the first scene I ever did for Nikos that influenced me most. Some background is necessary. I had been acting since I was five, starring in backyard plays, studying drama at the Arts Institute in my home town in Pennsylvania, and performing in school plays. When I was fifteen, a new community theater group formed in the city near my town, putting up ten productions a year, mostly musicals. For the next four years I was in just about every one of them, from which I mostly learned how to wear gold lamé and sell a song. Before transferring to NYU, I attended a small college in Allentown, where as a freshman I played leads in quite a few student productions, including (hilariously, at age eighteen) Nurse Ratched in *One Flew Over the Cuckoo's Nest*. With all this under my belt, by the time I got to NYU studying acting seemed not a chance to learn but to show off.

My first scene for Nikos was from *Hedda Gabler*. The class took place in the sprawling, decrepit rehearsal studio over the old Downtown Circle in the Square. I had learned my lines; I'd figured out the way I wanted to say them. I felt I understood something about the woman. After seeing some of the other scenes, I did think I had some things to show off. I felt I had a certain degree of stage presence some of the other students lacked, I had a sense of confidence and projected my voice well. I got up to do my scene.

I had barely begun when Nikos stopped us cold. I cannot quote him exactly but it went something like this: "Wait a minute. What do you think you're doing? You are not acting." I had not a clue what he meant. What had I been doing (all these many years!) if not acting? He continued: "You have not once looked at the other person in the scene. You do not know if he is happy or sad or if you have said something that affected him, and nothing he says changes you at all. You are saying lines and walking around, but it is like — you are completely disconnected. You are like — John the Baptist with his head cut off! Not only are you disconnected from your partner, you are disconnected from yourself! None of what you're saying means anything to you! You are more sophisticated than some of the people here, you know how to sit in a certain way in a chair, but that counts for nothing until you start acting. Forget it, just go back, bring it back again, rethink everything."

I had no idea what he meant. How could I have done over fifty productions and never acted? Perhaps I had no idea what acting was at all. I considered quitting. I kept bringing in scenes and Nikos kept shutting them down, telling me I wasn't "acting." "Go home," Nikos said, "and work on one line only. Do not think of *how* you will say that line. Think only of what you want to make your partner *do* when you say the line." So I did. Over and over and over, one line. And — as drop by drop, knowledge comes to the unwilling — it hit me. If I said the line with a certain intention, my partner responded by coming closer. And if I said it with another intention, he responded by walking away. I felt like Helen Keller spelling *water*.

Finally, I brought a scene into class from Ingmar Bergman's *Face to Face* — a short confrontation scene between a patient and an analyst, and my scene partner and I presented it twice, switching roles. I was terrified — I had never been on stage before without planning out in advance the way I would say and do everything. Nikos let both versions of the scene play through. At the end, he looked at me for a moment and said, "Okay, now we can start." And proceeded to tell me why my choices were wrong, why my behavior was wrong, and he went through a long list of other things my acting partner and I had neglected to bring to the work. After talking about our acting problems at great length, as an aside almost, he compared the two of us in the same role. "It's interesting, Andrea," he said to my partner. "You fought for yourself, but you didn't believe in yourself. And Jean, just the opposite, you believe in yourself, but you don't fight for yourself." It was the first of many off-the-cuff remarks he would make during my years of study that would inform not just my work, but my life.

All in all, taking the critique as a whole, the scene was a disaster. No matter. I was — for the first time — acting.

Part One
Beginnings: Bad Acting

> …My acting was meaningless! I never knew what to do with my hands. I didn't know how to stand on the stage, I couldn't control my voice. You have no idea what it feels like to know that you're acting badly!
>
> Nina, The Sea Gull
Anton Chekhov

ACTING ONE

Nikos' comments here focus on the fundamental tasks involved in starting the acting work. The first of these, Nikos suggests, is the actor questioning why she has chosen a particular scene to work on. Even in critiques on advanced work, this question, "Why are you doing this scene?" continually resonates — not rhetorically, but as a constant reminder to the actor that her own personal predilections and needs are the impetus for entering into the world of the play and the character.

NIKOS: Why do we do a scene? I'm basically saying that anybody can pick up any scene. But one person says, "Well, I'm attracted because the character does this," and another person is attracted because the character does that. "I'm attracted because in life I can never yell at anyone and in this scene I can." Or, "I'm attracted because I have all kind of demons in me and in this scene I can be sane." Or vice versa. Or someone says, "I want to do this kind of scene because I want to remake myself." We do scenes, we do parts, we do plays, as a sort of exorcism or escape or idealization. And I'm just not sure what either of you were responding to in yourselves when you decided to do this scene. Why this one and not a hundred others?

Consciously or unconsciously you have to know *why* you are doing the work. And it can't be just to act, just to demonstrate something. It can't just be: "I am in a scene class and so I have to do some scenes!" And later on, it can't be: "I do it because they are paying me." I mean, it will get bad because sometimes you will have to do things just because they are paying you! And then more than ever, you must find your reason. But in your work today, I had no idea what it was inside you that drove you to get up on that stage and walk and talk and say those words.

I don't understand, Gina, why you came in only to deal with the character's nervousness. And you kept dealing with nervousness over and over, so it really didn't matter what lines you had. Your acting was like seeing everything through thick, distorted glasses — you never saw colors, you never saw shapes. You seemed to have one need only: to show us that this character is nervous. But what's important for the woman in this scene is *not* dealing with nervousness, covering up that nervousness! Trying to hide the nervousness from him, trying to talk to him *without* nervousness. And Alex, all you were trying to show is that she didn't affect you. But, there was no reality between the two of you. I did not know why you were in the room together. Why didn't one of you just walk out?

MALE ACTOR: Well, my character is supposed to be indifferent to her —

NIKOS: But *all* you were playing was the fact that he was indifferent, which is already so clear in the lines, and which you made even more clear with your acting. Excruciatingly clear! And all she was playing was the fact that she was nervous. If I were you, I would've looked at her and said, "Boy, she's so nervous, I don't have to expend all that energy being indifferent! Because even if I smile at her and say something, she's so undone she can't even take it in." So why were you wasting all that energy being indifferent to someone who wasn't even noticing you!

And you kept repeating yourselves. You seem to assume, subconsciously, that the world is stupid, that what everybody in the audience wants and needs is some demonstration of some trait in the character that you must keep harping on and repeating over and over. You can't take all your lines and decide — "I'm going to play everything to show the peculiarity of the character" — because then you become like a stuck record. You were both stuck on demonstrating something you thought was the character. But remember, you never have character unless you're doing something to somebody else. It is not who you *are*, it is what you *do* that counts! You are nobody up to the time that you do something. If you just stand there your character is not revealed, right? Isn't that right? But if you say to him, "Come over here, I want to talk to you," you are saying something about the need of this character. If you say to her "get out of this room," you are revealing something else about the character. But you were not trying to affect each other. That did not seem to be the goal of your acting. Your goal, subconsciously, was to demonstrate something about the roles and because of that you were not using yourselves. Right now you sit here as yourself, you talk normally, now you sit in a normal way, but when you are acting, you start doing all these things that have nothing to do with your objective. You were using an unreal voice, you were using an unreal body, you were using an unreal image. Don't do that. Use only yourselves. The costume designer will dress you differently if the director wants to spell something different about the character. Or they'll cast a fatter person or a thinner person or a taller person. But you do not have to deal with those kinds of tricks.

If I asked the men in this room what would they do in life if they saw this woman acting that way, I don't think any one of them would want to have anything to do with her. And if I asked all the women in this room what they would they do with him, chances are the last thing they would do is stay in the room with him. Okay, tell me. What would the guys here do if you were in a room with her doing all those nervous things? No really, what would you do? In life! I don't mean on stage, because on stage anything goes, it's interesting, on stage we don't like to *see*, we don't like to *hear!* But what would you say to this girl you saw on stage just now if you met her in real life? If you were in that room with her?

MALE STUDENT: I'd tell her I had to go meet a buddy.

ANOTHER MALE STUDENT: I'd alert the authorities.

NIKOS: And leave! You know what I mean? You cannot afford to stretch credibility from the very, very simple things that spell reality up there. And the thing that spells reality is the fact that these two people are trying to move toward each other — even if they never really meet.

And we could ask the women the same thing. What would you do if you were in the room with him? Yes?

FEMALE STUDENT: Ask him to speak up.

ANOTHER: Grab him and say, "Look at me!"

NIKOS: You see? So you can't be metaphysical, you can't really say *how* you're acting unless you are doing the basics of acting. It doesn't really matter what you bring in for a character, the first thing is the communication between the two of you. The second thing is communication with a purpose. Communication with a purpose is followed by a reaction. And then reaction becomes reaction. And out of a highly specific way of doing and reacting we have character. But now we were not following that sequence of communication and reaction. Your acting decisions were *so* separate from the reality of each other, and from the reality of two human beings existing in the same world.

So do not try to do Acting II, or Acting III or Acting IV, unless you do Acting I, and Acting I is communicating, right? Even when two characters are not able to communicate, that doesn't mean they are ignoring each other. It's for you to take in what he's doing, hear what he's saying, and then react to it. But first you must hear it. If you don't hear it and you come in ready to pull acting trick number 222, the scene becomes repetitive and general and unreal. Unreal!

Don't be so eager to act. Don't do anything up on stage that you would not do with your husbands, wives, friends, relatives, or lovers, because it stretches credibility. If in doubt, ask always, ask somebody to look at you who doesn't know anything about theater and say, "What do you think? What would you do if I did this?" And if they say they would leave the room and it's not the cue to exit — well, you're in trouble.

THINKING VS. ACTING

The scene used as the canvas for the acting work here is the first scene between Stella and Stanley in Act I of A Streetcar Named Desire. *Nikos begins by reworking the scene and encourages the actors to deal accurately with the circumstances, to translate their thought processes about the scene into activities, and to explore for themselves their own personal reasons for playing the characters.*

NIKOS: The things you were *doing* in the scene weren't making any kind of sense in relation to the things that you were *talking* about in the scene. (*To the actress playing Stella:*) You were not protecting Blanche and you were not loving Stanley, and those are the circumstances of the scene. This is not up for grabs. This is not about choices or interpretation. This is about what the playwright gives you in the text and this is what you go to first.

Tennessee Williams gives you two things to deal with in this scene: the fact that you love Stanley and you don't want him to attack your sister. "I love you, but I don't want you to upset my sister." How would you say that? Just tell me, what do you do? (*The actress doesn't respond.*) Go ahead. Which way would you say it to him? Just say that line to him.

ACTRESS: (*Tentatively:*) "I love you, but I don't want you to upset my sister."

NIKOS: Okay, I didn't get one or the other. Do it again.

ACTRESS: "I love you —"

NIKOS: Don't get closer to him! Do it with your acting! Go ahead.

ACTRESS: "I love you, but I don't want you to hurt my sister'"

NIKOS: You see, I still don't get the love for him. Why don't you just say (*Nikos speaks forcefully and directly.*) "Look, I LOVE you, but DON'T HURT MY SISTER!" It's a very clear, open, line — why do you assume it should be said in a very cold voice?

The first time you did the scene you were trying to act by having feelings and thoughts about the scene, and I assure you that doesn't make any difference. It is not your *thoughts* or your feelings, it is what you *do* that counts. Stella's task in this scene is to get dressed, and you have to give yourself the kind of dressing activity that is interesting to you. Now it might be that you as a person love getting dressed up. Or it might be the way Kazan directed her — putting the lipstick on, which I am told involves a great deal of precision — makes you so clear and so precise that you don't want to get upset because you don't want to mess it up. You must try to find the kind of activity that makes sense to you and mirrors your objectives in the scene. But remember, thinking has nothing to do with acting! If acting were great thinking, we'd all be great actors! Yet I cannot act. I think about it, but I can't act. So don't assume that every time somebody thinks, it's acting. What you have to do is translate honestly the whole thought pattern into the activities. So you say, first you try the bracelet, then you try the necklace, and then you try the dress, and you try to find out which one of these activities feeds your objectives as the character.

Let me describe how your behavior in the scene was at odds with your words. First (*To the actress playing Stella:*) when you tried to establish the fact that you love him, you did that by getting very close and sexual with him, which certainly didn't make any sense! Because at this particular moment the last thing Stella wants to do is go to bed with that man. Stella wants to get dressed, make herself attractive, take her sister, and leave. "I'm here to tell you I must be going," in the words of Groucho Marx. And again, this is not interpretive. It is a given circumstance in the text.

Then Stanley came over to you and started asking you questions about Blanche, right? And your choice was that this made you totally upset, you tried to eat and you didn't eat, you tried to drink and didn't drink. Rather than playing (*Openly, warmly, with a bit of frustration:*) "This is just another, ordinary evening at home. What are you doing, sweetheart, why are you doing this?" All your lines are about "What's wrong? Why are you talking about?" so I don't know why you decided it would be best for Stella to have a nervous breakdown when he asked you about Blanche!

(*To the actor playing Stanley:*) Rick, I wish you would not go idle between lines. I mean it's amazing, she's hitting you with the lines, she's touching you and nothing affects you! You don't do anything until you get back to your lines! You can't do that, because in between you become blank. And then you have to take a lot of time to get the motor going again for yourself with each new line. Your through-line should be happening no matter what, your life in the scene should be happening no matter what. Your life changes by the fact of the impositions, but if I'm going to go out and cross 42nd Street I'm going to walk first. If it's windy I'll do it one way, if it's raining I'll do it another way, snowing another way, and if a lot of people are coming in my way, I'll do it another way. You know what I mean? But first I am going to walk across that street. You seemed to be expecting, somehow, for inspiration to hit you before you did anything.

Again, what is interesting in acting is not thinking but thoughts translated into behavior. For you, Stella, it's: "Let me investigate the two hundred ways that I bring this man around." And then for you, Stanley, it's: "Let me investigate how much resistance and how much nonresistance she has, let me investigate that if I touch her hair she reacts more, or if I look her in the eyes she reacts more." So, first it's getting your lives going, which are very clearly drawn by the play. Second is letting yourselves loose in your ability to *adapt* your way of dealing with the particular obstacles, to the interference that's coming at you. (*Dismissively:*) And, by the way, in a scene like this, like in life, people obviously want to interrupt each other, so just interrupt. You don't have to make those actor-interruption sounds, you know, where you make a little noise but really have no intention of saying anything!

And then more important, somehow, what kind of fascinates me, is that I wish I knew what both of you loved about those parts. Why are you going up and doing these roles unless you really love something about them? Is it because you love independence, is that why you love playing Stanley? Is it the fact that he's a macho guy, is it the fact that this woman adores him, is it the fact that he comes home and he's the king in his house? I mean, what is the thing that grabs you, Rick, and interests you and fascinates you in this?

And what is the thing that fascinates you in playing Stella? Is it the fact that you're taking care of your sister, that you're protecting her, the fact that Blanche was brought up, you know, in a great world, and she lost it and she's sad? And that you are not sad that you lost your world because you got Stanley? Is there something in the sensuality that you love? There are two million things for you to use as a springboard to act in a scene like this, and everyone finds different things about those parts. But you started playing Stella and I had the feeling that you were undone playing this part, that you hated something about playing her!

You've got to be up there because you love something in the role, or in the life of that person, right? Obviously, technically, it was a disaster because you had your thoughts, but you never really tried to say, "What can I do with my thoughts? Where can I take them, how can I play with them, how can I invest them?" But most important I think, there was nothing, really, that you loved.

You've got to help yourselves; you cannot wait and assume that you're going to get inspired. The second time you did the scene, you began dealing with each other. The sitting helped, the kneeling helped, putting the clothes in and out of the trunk, helped, right? Pulling him down helped, putting on clothes on helped, all these things helped you because what they do is convince the body. You know, tennis shoes, and three-inch-high heels make you walk differently. Acting is not a thought process, it's something that happens with the body. And what happens to the body ignites your acting mechanism.

BANISHING THEATRICALITY

In the following critique, Nikos is not gentle to the students whose work he has now seen a number of times. He exhorts them here to refuse to become enamored of a kind of theatricality that comes out of clichéd ideas about acting rather than the true circumstances of the scene, and he catalogues the variety of tricks that actors often insist on using, and the futility of doing so.

NIKOS: (*Speaking with much urgency and frustration:*) I am really not sure *why*. *Why* in this situation would you eat peanuts and why would you look at that flower? Why do you think it's so interesting to be adjusting the folds in your dress? I do not know why you really assume that these symbolic gestures of — whatever it is — class, manners, behavior are interesting. Or, I'll tell you what, if you think they're interesting, why don't you put them all together in a skit which would last about fourteen to fifteen seconds before you started repeating yourself? But don't do them in a whole damn scene!

In a scene where you are saying "I want to do this, I'm interested in you, look at me, I am in love with somebody, that person attracts me, I talk to you as a friend," in a scene where you're really saying some very interesting things about your life — why do you, Lisa, assume that all these little acting things should really distract you? I know why, because you for some reason or another, as I've said to you before, you assume that stupid things like that are interesting. They are not interesting, dear, unless somebody can do them brilliantly. You cannot do them brilliantly, so don't do them at all.

Sure, Kate Nelligan can pour the wine into the glass from two feet above and still hit the glass and pouring wine like that makes people applaud, but this has nothing to do with acting!* It's just a kind of an ability to perform certain tasks which a lot of other people who don't act can perform too, right? Things which you can do with a mask, which you can do in darkness — basically, magic tricks! But don't let these physical feats attract you more than the acting in the scene.

Remember what I've been saying to you about trying to *set* everything. You still have a problem working through the scene without knowing *how*

---

* *Nikos is referring to Nelligan's performance in David Hare's* Plenty.

you're going to say this line and *how* you're going to say that line, and that's why you miss lines. The reason you miss lines is that they're associated with a certain kind of bad behavior in your acting. Just assume, just say to yourself that all you have to do is say to him: "Listen to me." Right? It's very simple. (*Nikos speaks cleanly and urgently:*) "Please listen to me, I want you as a friend, I like a guy, I think I love him, no, I don't think I love him, listen, I am talking to you!" Take all of your lines as a monologue and you'll find out something very interesting about the part. You will find there is a through-line! But, why, *why*, in between all the lines do you just decide to quit your objectives and play with something? Playing with the peanuts and the brandy and the flowers and sitting around adjusting and draping your dress are symptomatic of the fact that you think those particular things are interesting! Well, they are not! They really are not. I mean, we have all seen these things over and over again and they are boring.

When Frank Langella came to audition for me, he did four lines, and I cut him off and said, "Great." He said, "What do you mean? I prepared — " And I said, "Listen I'm going to hire you." At that time he hadn't done anything, but after his four lines from Richard II, I knew I wanted to use him. Olympia Dukakis did the same, a very brief audition. I was very impressed with the way she was using herself. I hired Blythe Danner on that basis, too — I saw a clip from a movie that was maybe only a minute long or less. That's all I saw of her. But what I saw was an honesty, an honest use of her wonderful instrument. What else do you need?

You see, there's nothing left for you to use but your own emotions. Because the other things, other people have done them before you and they have done them in a more interesting way, anyway. A lot of people in musical theater do them and all the people in the Thirties movies used to do them, but now it's become almost like a takeoff you would do at a party, an imitation of an actress, of someone being 'actress-y.' Is that really how you want to invest your work?

When you were finally pinned down and when you finally allowed some of the frustration to come in, it started to be interesting. You were trying to reach him and it was truer. Even if a play is a comedy, it's a comedy because something real happens before or something real happens after the comic moment. And if you push it further you will find out the scene is about a woman who is trying to get a man who is madly in love with her to be her pimp, and that is very funny! With just a little adjustment it would have been a very funny scene. Why? Because then it would have been about your lack of awareness in asking somebody to do something that will screw up his whole life! It is your total lack, really, of perception and sensitivity to another person, of adjusting your own particular need ahead of his need, your insistence on that, that makes it funny — not the things you are doing with the peanut and the flower. It is the incongruity, really, of what he wants and what you want.

(*Nikos' voice rises with frustration.*) But something must be bad, Lisa, because I keep saying this to you over and over! I've said "cut it out" many times, and yet you go back to these things, even though you are perfectly capable of having some very true moments. Some of your moments connect, you were almost teary when you said, "I need something, I want to talk to you, please listen to me." Yet you insist on always going back to this fake thing! Don't be attracted to scenes by a peculiar set of manners. Be attracted by the peculiar set of circumstances.

Now, Tony, I thought you became much cleaner than I've seen you before, which was very good. But I wish that you did not have this determination to examine the floor! You really did nothing but look at the floor. And I kept looking at the floor because you were looking at the floor. And there was a mouse in this room yesterday so all I could think was that it came back! From a technical point of view it's tough because all the light is, you know, up there. I mean, there aren't footlights anymore, right? And from another point of view it was almost like saying, "Well, I now want to abdicate from dealing with what is interesting in acting." You were really minimizing your tasks as an actor.

The interesting thing would be to look at her. More interesting than that would be to look at her and try to convince her that you do not love her. Or to really deal with the fact that you're angry and then say, believably: "I am not angry." Those tasks take a certain amount of effort on your part. But instead you were assuming that most interesting is dealing with your thoughts, and it is not because that takes no effort. The tension is not there. Seeing something crooked and trying to straighten out is not there.

I don't know, I really do not know, why actors take a glass of brandy just to pour a glass of brandy! Rather than saying, (*With determination*:) "I'm going to drink it because I want to get drunk, because I'm upset." No, instead the actor toys with it. I really don't understand. You don't see that very often in real life unless somebody exaggerates something about their manners. You know what I mean? The way some people smell the corks of wine bottles and the corks don't smell anymore anyway! But we all know people who do that kind of a number to register that they know something that somebody else does not know. And I think if you go through all these rituals that people do in life you would find that most of them are not valid or authentic. These little rituals are just things that somebody once told them are kind of interesting. But as an actor you can't afford that. You really cannot afford to do takeoffs, or behavior that is almost imitating someone else's behavior, especially theatrical behavior that exists nowhere except as a cliché.

There are so many things the script allows you to do with the drink. I can see you smashing the glass, I can see you drinking it fast, I can see you trying to drink it and pouring it in the plant next to you. It was interesting, Tony, she gave a carnation to you which could've worked. If you had used it to build your frustration, your response might have been: "Goddamn it, do I need this carnation now?"

Guys, really, it stretched credibility. When the situations are interesting and strong, anything that clutters it works against you. Instead, pick up the tasks that help you as actors to use the maximum of yourself — to bring more out of your inner world. In this scene all you really have to do, Tony, is to sit a little bit further away, and for you, Lisa, go on your knees and say, "Help me, save me!" All it really needs is for you to grab him and take him outside and lean against the porch and tell him that. That would've been theatrical. But it's not theatrical because you're wearing these long black gloves or toying with a drink. That is just symbolic of being theatrical and it doesn't involve acting talent. It only involves a misguided tendency to pick up things and do things you have seen some place and associated with acting. Intensify ten times the need, then you have a chance of finding something fascinating for yourself. But the more you go into this little doodling the more you're hurting yourself. You're doodling rather than painting and it's bad doodling and it's unnecessary.

BOTCHED EXPERIMENTS

> *The scene in question (between Amanda and Laura) is from* The Glass Menagerie. *Nikos' comments, however, do not focus on specifics of the scene or the text itself, but on where the acting in any scene begins. He suggests that originality comes from a specific response to the other actors on stage and circumstances of the play, rather than from a decision to take an unusual approach.*

NIKOS: You both made a decision to make the scene experimental or unorthodox. But you were both trying to be unorthodox in exactly the same way, which is kind of contradictory! There was such a similarity in the things you were experimenting with. What I'm saying is this: It might be interesting for one of you to be wandering all around up there doing odd behavior, but not both of you. You know what I mean?

And I love those things. I love when I go into rehearsals and an actor says, "What do you think about tearing apart a pillow here?" It's great. But you can't give that to everybody because with four people on stage you will create identical quadruplets up there! One person does something and the other one responds to it. Unless you do that, as I've said many times before, the acting is totally eliminated.

When you experiment, you must do it for a reason, and with certain specific ingredients. In your efforts to find ways to trigger something in each other you must chose the kind of movement or the kind of blocking or the kind of physical tasks that are going to create within you something specific about the character's needs. If you decide to wander, or tear apart a pillow, you do it in order find something about that character. You couldn't find things out about these people in this situation because you took such a nonscientific approach in your experimentation. It was almost like acting exercises just for the sake of themselves. It was never, "If I lay down this way, if I deal with a particular physicality that way, it helps trigger something emotionally that is called for in the text."

I also found that you really did not need each other on that stage. You see, you said all those wonderful lines but you never said "Help me" to anybody. (*Nikos talks to the actress playing Amanda in the scene.*)I love that you got excited, Katie, because I haven't seen that from you. But take the moment that you say, "Do it." You said "Do it." — but then you turned away from her and you didn't get the payoff! The payoff is not saying "Do it." The payoff is that she *does it* when you say "Do it." You both seemed like very — and all the women are going to attack me — but you both seemed like feminists up there! You both enjoyed having a cause, and it didn't matter what the other person was going to do. It was never(*Imploringly:*) "I need you." It was, (*In a sharp, blustery voice:*) "This is who I am and this is what I'm doing." It was about competitive opinions, not about really needing each other. I'm not talking now about interpreting the material, because the material can go many ways. I'm just talking about the reality of what we saw.

It is not deciding to say a line in an unorthodox way that makes your acting original. It is only by taking things from each other and responding to them in your own unique way that you find an unorthodox, original way of dealing with the scene. I don't think that when you are rehearsing, at least at this stage, you should necessarily decide to do justice to the scene. I think you should do some scenes just for yourself, filter them through your own peculiar inner world, even if that goes 180 degrees against the text. Stretch the credibility of the scene, but never stretch the credibility of acting. Never stretch credibility in terms of your response to what the other person is doing.

You find out that a tremendous amount of time we get deceived by good acting. It's always fascinating to me when the critics say, "This production was wrong because of this and this and this." And they haven't really watched the acting up there. Rather than saying, "Well, their interpretation was totally different from mine, and what they worked on was wonderful, but my idea is that they should have worked on that and that." But really good acting can sometimes fool you into thinking that the text is about something you never even thought of.

Unfortunately, too much of theater criticism — or art criticism — involves people going in expecting something that they know or want, rather than dealing with what they *find*. And bad acting is like that too. Instead of dealing with what you *find* in the circumstances or in the other person, you deal with something in your mind about the character or about the play. And when you do that, you isolate yourself from the sources of your acting. You have no chance to do real acting when so much of it is predetermined.

ACTRESS: I tried not to think of the lines. I tried to do what you talked about with *Sea Gull*. I tried to — just pretend that it was one of these scenes where you've said — okay, just be physical. I somehow thought —

NIKOS: Well, why would I say to someone, be physical?

ACTRESS: Well, because I have a tendency to block and stage and think, oh I'll say it this way, or I'll say it that way. I didn't think about the scene, we only rehearsed it twice —

NIKOS: Well, I wish you'd think about the circumstances in the scene, that's what's interesting. I wish you'd think about the other acting on the stage, because that is interesting. Saying "I didn't think about the scene" is not what concerns me. What concerns me, is what *did* you think about? It is so interesting that actors always say: "I didn't want to do this, I didn't want to do that." You might *not* have done *this*, and you might *not* have done *that*, but what did you *do*?

I wonder why so many people say that, that's so interesting! I hear it so often, actors tell me things like, (*Proclaiming:*) "Well, I thought of not blocking it." Or, "Well, I didn't want to do a stereotyped version." I really know more about what people *don't* want to do than what they *want* to do. I go up to an actor and I say, "Why are you doing this?" And he says, "Well! The reason I didn't want to play this scene funny was because of this." And I say, "Wait, wait, wait, I wasn't really asking you to play the scene funny." (*As the actor, taken aback:*) "Oh, oh, I thought you were asking why I didn't want to do that."

It's interesting how people approach the work — even their lives, I don't know! — out of negative reasons. Like, "I don't want to appear weak, I don't want to appear mush, I don't want to deal with vulnerability, I don't want to deal with strength." Don't worry about what you don't want to deal with. By selecting certain things, just know what you *want* to deal with. If there is such an avoidance of doing things, of course nothing is going to happen for you.

You two, really, should have been irritated with each other. You should have been irritated, [*Amanda*] because Laura was doing all that stupid smiling and you should have been irritated [*Laura*] because your mother was such a killjoy! I don't even care if that is in the lines or not, I'm just dealing with the reality of the way you two appeared. You cannot not see something and pretend you are not seeing it. Because that is where the acting starts. Never stretch what you see because then you are in trouble, you know? I mean, what is that thing about great artists? It is not their hand, it's not they *draw* brilliantly, it is that they *see* brilliantly. They see, and then they respond. But the first thing is to be able to see.

SUGAR-COATING

> *In this critique of a scene from* The Killing of Sister George, *Nikos explores a variety of acting issues that he returns to in greater detail throughout. He talks about the difference between making choices and using circumstances; he pins down a definition of "moment-to-moment" work as well as going over tools for honing specificity in the work. He outlines the basics of script interpretation and suggests that good plays and good acting are based on an "exaggeration of human needs."*

NIKOS: We have to be very careful about this whole moment-to-moment thing that people talk about. You can say: "I play this moment, I play that moment, I play another moment," but that does not really mean that these moments should be uninformed. It does not mean: "I play a happy moment here, an unhappy moment next, a third confused moment there, and a cruel moment next." That is not playing moment to moment, that's playing contradictory things, you know?

What kind of amazed me about you both is that you would touch some material, some subject that was interesting, you would start using a color, and then you would immediately drop it. Why? In life you do not abandon completely the fact that you have one worry or problem to deal with something else.

The moment-to-moment work must be built on the circumstances, on certain 'givens.' In this scene some of the circumstances are that the character wants to dance in the ballet, that she is upset that she doesn't have kids, that she's worried that she's doing very neurotic things. Those are the given circumstances of the play and the circumstances do not *come in* moment to moment, they are *the basis* of your moment-to-moment acting. When you go into a play or a scene, you carry with you a palette of certain colors, and then you use those particular colors differently every time you paint. If you start embroidering something, you pick up certain threads to take with you, you have an idea that for this particular design you are going to use the white, the blue, and the green. What was amazing with the two of you is that you would do something and then you would shelve it completely. And then you would pick up something else, and then you would shelve that.

For example, the playwright puts liquor in this scene, but it is not there to show drunkenness. It is put there to color everything else. So that being upset about her job is colored by the liquor, and worrying about her friend is colored by the liquor, and being jealous is colored by the liquor. This is a simple matter of the two of you saying, "How do we *start* our acting," and I'll talk more about that in a moment. But first of all, you cannot deal with each subject as if there is no yesterday and as if it is not about to be around tomorrow.

Now, I'm not really asking for you to "color" the results of your acting. I'm asking you to color the moment-to-moment work of your acting with the original premise that you have chosen in the scene. The audience is not going to *know* what that is, but this will give specificity to your acting. You cannot give specificity to your acting just from your words, because words are not totally specific. For example, a wall. A wall means nothing until I try to fight against the wall, or until I get claustrophobic with the wall, or until I want to paint on the wall. But unless I have *a response* to the wall, the acting will lack specificity.

What you somehow have to do when you're up on that stage is to make conscious or subconscious decisions, not choices — you see, that's the bad thing, we now often use the word "choices" in terms of results, in terms of what things we choose to demonstrate about the role. So I am not talking about the choices you make, I'm talking about the choices that have *already* been made for you as far as the script is concerned. First you have to ask yourself what is already there. You must start from certain kinds of decisions, which then leave you free to create and to make the scene play on a moment-to-moment basis. These are not what people erroneously call "choices," because they are not decisions about how to act the role, they are specific information found in the text that give you the internal momentum to create life on the stage. Identifying these is how you start.

Take the liquor. A *choice* is saying to yourself that you want to make the other person completely drunk. But *the fact that you're drinking* is a circumstance which is written in the script. It is in the script that you keep drinking so that means you are sort of required to be constantly thinking, "I want to drink some more, I want to drink some more." And because the lines tell you that he wants to keep her here and he wants to love her, you need to keep that going within you, too: "I want to keep you here, I want to love you" — that is the refrain that keeps going through you as you act the scene. These things don't just come in with the lines, when you actually *say* "I want to keep you here, I love you." These things are the refrain, the melody between verses that makes the song.

Take the line, "I want to drink something." Holding a bottle and pouring when you say that is not interesting. But picking up the bottle when the line is "Remember when I came to the bathroom and it was all steamy" — that's the time to drink, to deal with the bottle. The time to drink is on a line like "No, these pills are wrong." The time to mess up the pills is when you remember her in the bathroom. The time to deal with the fact that she's a lesbian is not on the lines about that but when something else puts you on spot.

You both refused to pick up the emotional elements in the scene that would trigger a very prejudicial, specific point of view in you. As characters it's almost as if you have to see everything through a very specific pair of glasses, so to speak. The glasses are colored a particular color and so everything to you looks green. And because you see certain things green when the rest of us see beige, we begin to get a sense of who you are as the character.

You also refused to do certain things called for in the scene, which makes it tough for you. I mean, it's tough to do this scene unless you deal with wanting to drink, not because you should play it drunk, but because that *need* for the liquor throughout is necessary. You refused to do the undressing in the scene. Obviously this is a scene about a woman taking off her clothes and a man watching. It's a sexual scene, and that is what drives him crazy, looking at this very young girl-child, with her underpants on — not blue jeans and boots. He's turned on, and you as the character have to go and deal with that. If you don't want to deal with these things, pick another scene to do, but if you pick this one you have to go for it. You have to do something to give yourselves, not us, *yourselve*s, the feeling of danger.

You eliminated the problem of sexual conflict, but actually, you eliminated many problems from the scene. What worries me always is when the acting seems to be cleaner than life, you know? It really doesn't work. Because I don't know anyone who talks or does something without a reason. You say to yourself, "I wonder why this person did that, or why this person did this." Some people try to impress you, some people try to reject you, somebody comes in to take a letter for you and you realize that their mind is not in the letter, that they are totally out of it! But it always fascinates me how people in life can be more interesting than the people on stage. I mean, you can go to Bloomingdale's and you can see who wants to be the boss, and who wants to get out of Bloomingdale's, and who wants to pick up somebody and escape. You can go to bars and see the way people order drinks or the way people turn and talk to you, how they behave and why they behave that way. You know what I mean? And yet we don't see half of that on stage, ever.

A cab driver brought me up here today, a lady. I think really I should give this to a comedian to do as a monologue. This lady started off, she said, "I'm sixty-three, thirty-seven years in New York. Goddamn it, look at all those freaks, look at all of those freaks! First thing I'd do in New York is build jails. Second I put all of them in. What do you do?" I said, "I teach acting." She said, "Oh boy, I hope you don't teach for that Lee Strasberg guy." I said, "He's dead." She didn't hear me. She went on attacking Lee Strasberg. She would change the subject but every three sentences there was an attack: "Drugs, that's what it is about Strasberg, drugs, I bet." Eventually she told me that she used to work in the Police Department and she had to leave at the age of sixty and so that was why she was driving a cab, but every day she wished she was back at the Police Department so that she could get all the drug addicts in New York City. "Those sons of bitches, those sons of bitches," she kept saying. And apparently Lee Strasberg was one, too. And I kept saying, "He's dead!" But she didn't hear. Then she said, "See my hair, see my hair?" And I said, "Yeah?" and she says, "Your hair is white. See, I have no white, none whatsoever." I said, "Yeah, that's great." "Well, that's because I dye it," she said. And in between she kept singing — "If you can make it here, you'll make it anywhere, New York, New York," and then back to attacking Lee Strasberg and New York! And at the end when I gave her a tip, she says in a little voice, "God bless you!"

What I'm saying is, something in what she was doing and saying compels you to wonder what happened to her! And after a while you see that she was obviously very upset about leaving the Police Department, and everything else that came out — about the hair, or the jails, or even Lee Strasberg — had something to with the underlying thing she was upset about. Every three lines or every five lines or every seven lines, it just came out. And I think it's kind of fascinating that we look at people in the streets and our fantasy and our imagination sparks about what these people are doing. But on stage, often, it doesn't.

On the stage we get so involved with — not the moment-to-moment, but the sentence-to-sentence. Moment-to-moment does not mean that in moment "A" you forget the love that you have, and in moment "B" you forget the need that you have, and in moment "C" you forget the rejection. These things run throughout. For example, in *A Streetcar Named Desire* obviously Stanley and Stella are two people who love each other and have a history with each other. Now, they can be fighting, they can be dealing with the food, they can be dealing with dressing, they can be dealing with anything, but all of their moment-to-moment activity must be in proper perspective to the given circumstances.

The final thing is, I'm amazed that we are picking scenes that are frightening in terms of their life expectations, and we are really sugar-coating them. I mean, actors are supposed to be doing the opposite, actors are supposed to look at an innocent baby and assume it is a monster! You know? They're supposed to be like Hedda Gabler: "You touch my hair? No, I burn your hair!" How can we take scenes like this, where someone has somebody kiss the hem of her dress and chew burnt cigars, and make that so gentle and innocent that it becomes a text for Julie Andrews! I don't understand it!

Actors are supposed to take material that is very safe and Pollyanna-ish and make it tough, but instead you took material that has all these impositions and you toned it down so much! I never saw the possibility of anybody grabbing anybody, the possibility of running away, the possibility of wanting to strangle somebody and then having to embrace them, or wanting to push them on the couch. I never saw the possibility of a rape or of a killing up there. And because of that, it was not particularly interesting. It's not that those are the only two subjects, because I'm not even talking about subjects, I'm talking about the potential of losing control, one way or another, either in the sense of a big embrace or of an attack.

So. The first thing you have to do is intensify the degree of importance, the degree of turbulence, the degree of, almost, prejudice that connects you. The second thing is that you got to get life from all over. I mean if the script calls for somebody to really pull down the blue jeans, or put on stockings, or whatever, you have to do it. If the script calls for drinking the liquor, if it calls for you pushing her down on the floor, you must go further. Spill the pills so they have to go all over the floor which would infuriate her, put a big object in your bag so that he can't get close to you, play with the dolls, take the dolls away, spill the ice cubes. Just find things that by reacting and responding to them, you can create acting from them.

As I think I've said many times, you go out there and you have a portmanteau, you have a suitcase and you pick up certain things to wear and you wear them. I don't mean literally, I mean figuratively. You pick up things like "angry at this person," "desperately in love with this person," "possessed by this person." You pick up things that make you respond, and usually they are explicit in the text. You pick up things like, "Every time I see red I get furious; every time I hear loud music I scream, every time I eat this, I throw up; every time somebody mentions the word joy, I jump." You know what I mean? You take clues from the text and connect them to things in yourself and then you bring them with you on stage so that when the other person does something you get to respond. What happened now was a series of, like, forty-two unrelated things which were kind of interesting, but they couldn't be sufficiently engaging because moment "B" was contrary to moment "A." And each moment was contradicting the previous moment rather than building on it. And because of that you really lost me.

My suggestion is when you do scenes like this — even when you're not doing scenes like this imagine that they are scenes like this! — but when you *do* do scenes like this, go out all the way because this is, you know, interesting territory. It's the apotheosis of people who socially are what somebody calls "normal," whatever that may be. Because you can't have theater with normal people. If Willy Loman doesn't get any contracts and he's old and he doesn't want to recognize it and he fights it, you have a play. If he's old, and doesn't have any contracts and he decides to recognize it and retire in Florida, there would be no *Death of a Salesman*. If Blanche in *Streetcar* says, "Well, I'm sorry, I'll stay out of your way, Stanley, I will not drink, I'll keep my hands off boys and I'll go back to my little room," she'd be okay. She'd get her pension and there wouldn't be a play.

The play comes in, the players come in, the scenes come in because of what some people would call weaknesses or indulgences, but we have learned to define as the exaggeration of certain human needs. Right? Which are out of proportion with somebody else's needs. And that's what really happens in all good plays. If you just love someone simply, without wanting to do anything with your love, you don't have a play. If you love and the other doesn't, then there's some kind of a conflict. There's always some kind of "I want to do this but I cannot do that." Or, "I feel, but I need." Or, "I want to cry but I can't." Until those things are there — well, even if they're not there in the material, put them there.

And equally important, find what you touch back to as the center of your world and then go ahead with your lines. Go back, touch it, and then come up with the lines, touch it again and then go back to the lines. "I need you, let's make love;" "I need you, let's drink;" "I need you, why are you going;" "I need you, the doorbell is ringing." If you see everything in relationship to that center then you are okay, but if you don't, then you move through all the territory of the play with your work changing on a dime, which shows that you don't depend on anything. And therefore you have no right to act. Because if you don't depend on anything, then you're *creating* your own acting rather than the acting *emerging* subconsciously out of needs which cannot be completely justified, clarified, or fulfilled. But by making those constant adaptations, as you did, you lose your life, your personality, your need, and your work becomes a kind of social statement rather than a real one.

COMMENTARY
BY JOANNE WOODWARD

> *Joanne Woodward, a star of stage and screen for forty years, began her directing career at the Williamstown Theater Festival in 1988. As an actress, she played the leading roles in Nikos Psacharopoulos' productions of* The Glass Menagerie *and* Sweet Bird of Youth. *For WTF she has directed* La Ronde *and Clifford Odets'* Golden Boy, Rocket to the Moon, *and* The Big Knife, *among others.*

The following is excerpted from a conversation with Ms. Woodward that took place in Williamstown, soon after the opening of her production of The Big Knife.

My most overwhelming experience with studying with someone was Sandy Meisner. He was tough, as Nikos is here, but I think that's probably a good thing. At the time, of course, I thought it would simply destroy me. I remember an improvisation I did in Sandy's class. I had to come into an office and say to another actor — Arch Johnson, this big Irish actor — I had to come in and tell him (*In a tearful, melodramatic voice:*) "Your brother has made me pregnant and I need money for an abortion!" And I made my entrance and said the line, and Arch — wisely — laughed at me! That was not what I expected! I became so undone by his reaction that immediately I burst into tears. The first half of the improv I was just "acting." But the minute he started to laugh my reaction became so physical and so emotional. I cried, I staggered around the room, I tried to figure out what to do, couldn't, and then abruptly ran out the door! I stood outside sobbing and sobbing in the lobby. Finally someone came and got me and said "Sandy says you have to come back." So I came back in and stood on the stage and Sandy looked at me for a very long time, holding his cigarette, and said, "Well, Joanne. That's the first truthful thing you've done this year."

I felt as though I'd been stabbed to the heart. I didn't take it for what it was, which was — "Hey, I really took a big step." I took my courage in both hands and went to him, telling him how scared I was that he'd said that, that I felt afraid to do anything for fear that it wasn't going to be truthful. And he looked at me and he said, "You know something? When you start to play the violin you have to learn where you put fingers on the frets. You can't see where the notes are, it's not like a piano, it's not immediately evident. You have to sense it, you have to feel it, you learn to know." And then he said, "I tell you, it takes about twenty years to know where to put your fingers." And he was right. I didn't feel like I found my fingering to my own satisfaction until I did *Rachel, Rachel,* which was many, many years later.

The greatest direction Nikos ever gave me was when we did *The Glass Menagerie.* Now, some people have no problem with accepting notes from a director. And I admire them. I'm not one of them. To this day, it's very difficult for me — my husband and Nikos are two of the most difficult! I'm very bad at being directed. I'm always somewhere else, my stomach is churning, I'm trying to find some way to keep it my own — and so I probably wasn't listening intently to what he was saying. Finally he lost his cool and he just looked at me and yelled "Joanne, Joanne! Do it like this, like this!" and he acted it out, not the words, but physically. He stopped trying to explain and he just — showed me. And I looked up at him and thought "Oh! Yeah! Right!" I got it. What he showed me, in a physical way, was the directness of her. No thought, no calculation. Nothing in the way of her response. At the time, I wasn't ready to do it that way — to play the *meanness* of her, the drive of her, the *really* dark side of her. He tried to talk to me about this other side of her, but I think he saw that the explanation wasn't reaching me. So instead he gave me one physical thing that spelled the emotion.

The thing that fascinated me about Nikos was how he brought it to the body. That a certain kind of physicality indicated — for want of a better word — the emotion, the intention he was striving for. I find that's what I do now when I'm directing. For instance, when I was directing *Golden Boy* at Williamstown — I don't know, you get directorial moments, ideas that stick in your head. I wanted to find a moment in the last act about what happens with shock. What happens when something so awful, so shocking happens that you can't conceive of it. And around this time, my dog got killed. I was in rehearsal and Paul didn't want to tell me, but knew that I was coming home and he had to. And so he took me aside and sat me down and said — "Honey, I have to tell you —" I was eating an apple — "I have to tell you that

Ernie got hit by a car." I was sitting, and I had no idea how this happened — I was about to take a bite of the apple and I simply fell forward. I didn't faint, I just — everything let go and I fell to the floor. So cut to the last scene in *Golden Boy*, the scene where they're all gathered together in the living room and they get the phone call that the two other characters are both killed. And I needed something for the actor who was playing Tom Moody. So, I said "Could you just — fall down? Just let your legs go?" And he did it! It was an emotional moment translated physically — something Martha Graham used to talk about a lot. And did Nikos *approve* of that! He didn't ask me where I found it. He just said, "That moment — I love that." And I understood that he understood what I was looking for. It was my first time out, and I had no idea how to help an actor get to such a big emotion. But with that physicalization, you didn't even have to feel anything, you just had to do it. And it said everything.

Golden Boy, at Williamstown, was the first time I'd directed with the grown-ups! I went to Nikos, and told him I wanted to try something, maybe some scenes with the apprentices and he said "Why don't you do a play?" And I said, "Oh, I don't know!" and he said, "Oh, yes you can, you can do it!" I picked *Golden Boy*. I leapt into it, I did everything I thought you were supposed to do, but of course I had no experience. And Nikos was extraordinary in that he left me to my own devices, left me completely alone for the first week. I was terrified, but so far nobody was leaving, the actors hadn't yet walked out! Nikos came in just about the time we got on the stage. He stood in the back, and I was, of course, very nervous. Finally he said, (*With a Greek accent:*) "I think I help you." He didn't say a word about the acting. He just sort of whispered in my ear about where they should *be* onstage. And I didn't really understand what he was doing, but I thought, well, I'm sure he knows what he's talking about. But after I did it, I looked and I said, "Oh, I see — then she's in focus here and he's in focus up there," and suddenly the stage came alive for me.

Golden Boy was the only time — sadly — that I directed when Nikos was alive. I've often thought of his passion for Chekhov. And every time I think, "Oh, I'm not going to do any more Odets," I end up going back to look at a play like *The Big Knife,* and I think, "No, there's something there, there's something that really touches me and affects me." *Rocket to the Moon,* which I also did here is another. And I've often though, "I wish Nikos was here, because he would understand my obsession with this!" I mean, people laugh, they say, "Joanne! What is it with you and Odets?" And I don't know what it is but it's something in me that inevitably attaches to that playwright. I feel like Nikos would've given me permission — "You do this, you go right ahead." It's a passion, it's like Joseph Campbell says, "Follow your bliss."

Nikos gave me these opportunities with such faith — which is another gift. I think one of the most extraordinary things about him was that he gave actors faith that they could do it. It was very gutsy on his part. That's the thing that I hold onto, and I never want to direct an actor in whom I don't have faith, because I think it would show. Sometimes you get actors who are not great actors, but if the connection is there, somehow you can give them the gift of saying, "I believe in what you can do. Do it."

PART TWO
Pitfalls

…let your own discretion be your tutor: suit the action to the word, the word to the action; with this special observance, that you o'erstep not the modesty of nature: for anything so overdone is from the purpose of playing, whose end, both at the first and now, was and is, to hold, as 'twere, the mirror up to nature; to show virtue her own feature, scorn her own image, and the very age and body of the time his form and pressure.

Hamlet
William Shakespeare

USING LANGUAGE

A scene from Bertolt Brecht's play In The Jungle of Cities *serves as a springboard for a discussion about approaching textual language in various genres. Nikos suggests that the actor's task when working on non-naturalistic material is to discover the underlying "life" that necessitates the form.*

NIKOS: I didn't get it. I mean, what were your thoughts? What were you trying to do? As you know, I don't usually ask actors to talk about the scene because I think the work should speak for itself. But I really didn't get this at all.

ACTOR: I wanted the scene to have a sort of expressionism —

NIKOS: But that is nonsense. You don't give it expressionism, it *is* expressionism because the scenes are short. Brecht is Brecht because of that. That's like saying that when you do Shakespeare you want to be poetic, and when you do Chekhov you want to be moody!

ACTOR: No, I didn't want the character to be poetic or moody —

NIKOS: That's not what I'm saying. I'm saying that you were atonal in this and you should not be, the way you should not be poetic in Shakespeare. In Shakespeare you should talk as if poetry was the only way possible to speak, you should use iambic pentameter the way everybody else uses language regularly. But don't assume because you have a play where the sentence structure is slightly peculiar for you, that your job as an actor is to sound like you're really underwater! Don't ever assume you have to change the acting form in order to get something out of the scene.

When the language of the text is different from the language you use in life you must find a way to make it *just* as natural for you, not similar, but *just* as natural. The way somebody sings well — it's like talk, only it's singing. Rather than exaggerating the artificiality of putting words to music, you do the opposite. I think the more exaggerated the form of an art is, the more organic the acting has to be. You were so abstract, you were so atonal, it's as if you assume that the interesting thing in the material is the form and it is not! What's interesting is the *life* which *necessitates* that kind of form.

When you act in a Greek play, obviously it's not about a peculiar kind of delivery, but about somebody's pain being so great that they cry out *"Ooooooooooooh!"* rather than "Oh!" But it doesn't mean because it is a Greek play the "Oh" should be done in a stylistic way, a "Greek" way, whatever that may be. It means that *the feeling should be exaggerated in order to meet the form.* The language comes out of some need, and then the words might become (*Each word forceful and elongated:*) "*Take this! And this, and this!*" Rather than (*Quickly, casually:*) "Take this and this and this and this." If you say it that way, without an emphasis that comes from a need, it makes the repeated words unnecessary. And consequently it becomes peculiar that the word *"this"* is repeated. A form is repeated only because there's some kind of an essence to it. It might be repeated because it is some kind of ritual, it might be that it is poetry, it might be that there is a kind of agony that drives it, but the form the language takes exists because of the underlying need, and serves the scale of that need.

You see, you had a line, "How lovely, it's the moon, it's red." It's not (*Nikos says the line atonally, with no punctuation.*) "How lovely it's the moon it's red." As if you assume there is something peculiar in saying it's a red moon. What's peculiar is the fact that this particular person chooses to express this feeling at this particular moment. I agree with some of the comments, there was a certain strength to you which I really enjoyed, but many times you're not working during the text. You're working before the text, or you're working after the text and that is wrong.

That's why, for instance, the best people to work with when you're doing a play are those actors who have a tough time with lines and therefore put in their own words and try to make sense of the lines as they speak them. So that the *line* becomes active, rather than the *feeling* about the line. Because you were mesmerized by an attitude, you were not really using the words as if you had never used them before.

Take the line "Look, look, Marie, there is something on your lip." What is it? What was the word?

ACTOR: Blister. "It's red but there's no blister."

NIKOS: Does he want her to have a blister, or doesn't he want her to have a blister? Is he accusing her or is he praising her? I had no idea what that sentence was doing except that you were trying to let us know it was a peculiar sentence. (*Nikos whispers:*) "No blister." I mean, it's a good translation, "*blister*" has a sound to it that's interesting. But you made the "*no*" and the "*blister*" the same sound.

The crazier the material is, the more logical you have to make it. I think this is the basis of all politicians, that's why they get elected. If you really take some of the lines these guys say and go back and read them, you say forget it! But they have the ability to communicate something that is so much more interesting than the words — with the emphasis just on the right word, with just the right attitude toward the activity that is *represented* by the inadequate words.

But here it was like a sound track running on one level and the scene running on another, and therefore the scene felt like it was dubbed. You really did, you sounded like you were trying to catch up with the visual. Don't ever violate punctuation. Don't ever be idle during the delivery of any line, even the shortest possible line. Now sometimes, this can be dreadfully overdone, like the way the late Geraldine Page just killed that revival of *Blithe Spirit* because she assumed she had to work with each word separately, and she was always hitting the wrong word. So you couldn't really get what Coward was doing. But most of the time it *is* making sense out of each sentence and having a purpose with each sentence.

You know, you can't be melancholic with Chekhov, you can't be lyrical with Williams, you can't be poetic with Shakespeare, and you can't be expressionistic with Brecht. You certainly cannot try to show Brecht's alienation effect by having two people who can't make sense of each other! It is the structure of the play, it is the activities of the play, it is the life of the play that spells alienation, not you trying to "act" alienated!

Remember, I'm not talking about your thoughts about the *play*, I am just talking about thoughts about the *form* of the play. Try assuming that this is a perfectly normal scene that happens to you every day on 42nd Street. It's just like a painter! A painter paints a red sky and if you ask him "why?" he says, "Sure, it's a red sky." But he didn't make it red in order not to paint it blue, he's doing it because he sees it red, and that red is perfectly natural to him. You made a strong decision about the language and the form and what that meant to you about expressionism. As I said, that's the worst. I go back to Greece to look at a Greek play and I can't even hear what they're saying, I really can't. Because there's just too much of an awareness, the way they do it there, that it *is* a Greek play, you know what I mean? So the actor who's the head of the Greek National Theater goes, (*Nikos' voice rings out atonally, in a declamatory, unnatural way:*) "And now I will go there and tell all my friends —" and you just say, "*What? What?!*"

There is just an assumption that because it is poetic language or Greek language or exaggerated language, it should be delivered only in one way. The same thing with Shakespeare. Everyone is just bending backwards to do the damn thing in a poetic way, so much so you don't even know what they're saying! You do not know what people are saying, because they're so aware of *how* they're saying it. It's just like the way people do the Chekhovs, there is that (*In a mournful, breathy, melancholic tone:*) "Oh, yeah. No. Why. Uh. Ee. Ah." And you say "What is going on?!" And somebody says, "Well, I did it that way because the play's about the inactivity or the melancholia," or something like that. Somewhere or other, in some esoteric way, the play might have something to say about that. But that doesn't mean you play that!

And you put so many — nonpregnant! — pauses in the scene. You must never allow the form of the material to stop the life of the material. And that's what you were doing. You thought about an "air" for the scene, a feeling for the scene, a mood for the scene. Instead of saying, "I'm going to catch that mood with active pieces of life that I will bring together," you just become moody. It was like (*Nikos speaks monotonously, flatly:*) "The words are not important, and I am not using them." You lost the text, and because of that you lost the reality.

CHARACTER CRUTCHES

Here, Nikos examines the ingredients of "character" work. He exhorts his students not to "impose" external characterizations but to "suspend" some of who they are to allow the character to emerge through specific elements of their own personalities.

NIKOS: Why did you decide to find so much outside of yourselves in order to create these characters? The things you picked up looked like they were superimposed, the voice, the gestures, all of it. And these things might be interesting for the play, but they were not really helping you as actors.

You were using certain character traits as crutches. Now it probably gave you a certain freedom. But when you find that kind of freedom through an element that's imposed, through a character element, it's like seeing everything through a scrim. You didn't lose a sense of the play, really, I thought you did justice to the scene. I just didn't think you did justice to yourselves.

I think both of you have learned to borrow things from images you have about the characters, or from the interpretive elements, which do not allow the natural juices to flow. I mean, Isabelle, your voice went up and down, sometimes it was loud and sometimes it was soft, but there was always a kind of imposition that you used with the language, so the character you created was really stronger than you in this situation.

I always think the whole idea of using yourself within the given circumstances of the play is much more interesting. I wish you had said, "We're not going to do the scene, we're not going to do the play, but we're just going to use ourselves." Instead of focusing on the idea of *creating* a character, look into the area of *suspending* some of who you are but still using your own ingredients as people, of sifting the part through the sieve of who you are. It got impersonal, as if your work was saying, this is *somebody's* anger, and this is *somebody's* fear. I just don't know why you feel you have to hide yourselves so much rather than finding the character through yourself. It's the wonderful thing about George C. Scott. You see him in a play like *Present Laughter* and it's fascinating because he's not trying to do someone's else's version of *Present Laughter,* he's doing the George C. Scott version of *Present Laughter*.

You see this big man who is doing all those little things that we're used to seeing much more calligraphic actors do, and he does those things, but with the sense of being true to his own needs.

It's never really interesting to see somebody as Blanche in *A Streetcar Named Desire*. It's never interesting to see four apples. It is only interesting to see Cezanne's apples. Or somebody else's apples. With Blanche, it's interesting to see Dianne Wiest's Blanche versus, let's say, Carrie Nye's. Because Carrie Nye's Blanche is her own Blanche, not an archetype of Blanche. Why do people assume there is somehow, somewhere, an archetype, a goal for each character in a play? You see, nothing is really interesting about a mannerism that is borrowed from someone else or from your image about someone else. There is only something interesting if it is your own manner of doing it. It becomes a mannerism when it is repeated because of a certain obligation rather than because of a certain necessity. I'm not saying not to attempt the external character — I mean, Meryl Streep certainly is often behind some sort of an accent or behind some kind of physical thing that gives her freedom, that works well for her. At the same time she was most interesting to me in *The Deer Hunter* where the performance was less spectacular but had more reality to it. So it was more moving. Do you know what I mean?

ACTRESS: Yeah, I do, but I'm curious as to what you're saying. You want us to say, okay, don't think about the play, don't think about the characters, just do it as an exercise to use ourselves?

NIKOS: No. I'm just saying find your *own* toughness, find your *own* lack of intelligence, if that's what you're playing, rather than assuming that those things come from talking in a certain way. I've been listening to forty-six Stanleys* and most of them come in and underneath

---

Auditioning for Nikos' 1988 production of A Streetcar Named Desire *at Circle in the Square.*

it all, they're still trying to find something of the same way that Brando did it. And you see somebody who is a totally different person trying to be like Brando, and you just say, "Please! Brando was Brando and therefore it worked but with you it is a reproduction, it is not original!" How would *you* get angry at this person, how would *you* do the activities, that's what's interesting, rather than copying either an actor who has done it, or a version of what is somehow in your mind. Because that limits you. It's not that the so-called "character" shouldn't come out, but that you let the character come out in a much more effortless way.

Occasionally the scene got showy in terms of what you were *expecting* the scene to do, rather than what you were *allowing* the scene to do. When you do scenes in workshops or classes, don't feel so much this obligation. I don't really mean that you should eliminate the play, but don't feel more of an obligation to the play than to yourself. Isabelle, it's interesting, when you had the anger it was good. But some of the pain didn't come out, or some of the problem didn't come out, or some of the vulnerability didn't come out because of the fact that you were hiding behind the mask of that character. And I think, Barry, there's much more talent there than appears to be. I think perhaps you get shy about that and maybe that's why I have a feeling you're hiding behind the mask.

ACTOR: I wish I had heard that direction before I started. I saw someone on the street that I based the character on. I said, "This is it" and I wasn't even aware of how much I was doing it. I guess that's why I need direction, because I couldn't see — "

NIKOS: But that's not what I'm saying, it's not a "direction." I mean, Chris Walken does something with his shoulders that everybody does a takeoff on later, some people say it's a 'mannerism' because they don't like him doing that, but it's not, because it's so much a part of him, he does it all the time. But if anybody else tries to do it, it's just funny, it becomes the musical comedy version of Chris Walken! With anybody good that you work with, after a while you find out there are things they do, things that people do takeoffs on at parties! Which is sometimes unfair, but the point is, these things are *theirs* rather than borrowed from somebody else.

If you don't find these things inherently in yourself, if you want to pick up something to use for the character — which I'm not saying you shouldn't do — then it should be the so-called the psychological gesture, the PG, that Michael Chekhov uses. Like if somebody's shoulder has been carrying an accordion or whatever, and then there is a pain that they are dealing with. Or if somebody doesn't want people to look at him, there's a kind of slight turning away which becomes a trait for the character. But try to make those things happen in such a way that they are elements of substance rather than elements of form. This work to me was an element of form, it was not happening like — like the way I move my hands. I move them a little too much, and people say, "You move your hands too much," but you know, to me, I just move my hands! It's not like I decide, at this particular moment I do this gesture, and at this particular moment I do that.

For both of you, I think the work is verging on good, and you really do not have to do these obligatory things. You might feel better using the obligatory things, but you don't need them. You know? That's why I said they're crutches. And I think that the moments that you were allowing yourselves to be yourselves — the grabbing and the pushing and the throwing of the shoe — were wonderful, I guess because

I didn't predict it, I didn't know that it was going to happen. It came out of something that was happening on the stage rather than coming out in regular intervals in order to demonstrate your ideas about the character to us.

Use your own voices, assume that this language is the way everyone talks, the way that you talk, and the scene will be much more interesting for you. Forget about what you have to do to serve us or the play or anything like that. Make it interesting for yourselves and it will do that.

SEXUALITY AND DANGER

> *In this opening scene from Strindberg's* Miss Julie, *Jean (a servant) and Miss Julie (the aristocratic daughter of a count) have a dangerous encounter on Midsummer's Eve. Nikos zeroes in on the risk in the scene, the sexual tension between the two characters, and the need for actors in scenes like this to "let their blood interpret" for them rather than their intellect.*

NIKOS: You weren't challenging each other! It was, as Stanley Kowalski would say, "We had this date with each other from the beginning!" The scene was all about two people with so much innuendo in their voices! As if you were both saying with your acting, "Guess what the two of us would be doing right now if only the damn playwright had given us an earlier cue to leave the room!" It became so flirtatious that it was annoying, you know? It was flirtatious, but it was without sexual tension. I got the feeling that if Jean and Julie left the room they were going not to have sex but, I don't know, to play with balloons, or something!

You missed the sexual tension, because sexuality expressed as flirtation isn't interesting. In material like this sexuality is never interesting unless there is some kind of conquest, unless somebody is conquering somebody and somebody is having a struggle. Now it can go either way, it can be her struggle or it can be his struggle, but one of you has to be stronger and one weaker so that the other person can try to work and chip away at the resistance. Or, on the other hand, the strengths of the characters need to be different. Jean is strong in one way, and Julie in another.

I agree with some of the comments, Jeff. I thought this was the cleanest acting I've seen you do. It was great to watch you not do what you've done in the past — which is, you get the ball and you look at the ball and you decide, (*Slowly and laboriously:*) "Now, this is a ball and I have to throw it and which way shall I throw it?" Because by that time you have lost energy to do anything. So the fact that you were more immediately responsive made you, for you, formidable. You were dealing with your self and your work in a new way and I thought that was kind of wonderful.

But Anna, I think your whole sense of the part was off. It is not about flirtatiousness, it is about a woman with needs. This woman obviously needs something desperately and her only way of getting it is by commanding. It is the only way she knows. Unlike St. Joan who hears her voices from God, this lady obviously hears her voices coming from her body! If you could allow those voices to be stronger, if you could allow the physical need to come out, and if you could allow the need to be imperious to come out, you would find out something about the scene.

She says, "Kiss my foot. (*Nikos is forceful and draws out the words:*) COME ON! NOW!" That line should feel like it takes five or ten minutes, you know? Don't throw something like that away. And Jeff, also unless you do something like bite that boot, the scene is not interesting. Just kissing that little boot is certainly a token gesture that anybody can do. But obviously it is more than a kiss, there is something sexual going on. If that's not there, it doesn't work.

I think the trick is that you've got to enjoy your own arbitrariness. So it becomes (*Speaking randomly, freely:*) "I am the person I am, I can use a whip, I can drop somebody, I can pick up somebody," (*Yelling:*) "SIT DOWN!" (*Then, whispering:*) "If I order you." So what really happens is the idea of possessing, the idea of controlling, the idea of becoming sexually involved with him acquires many more colors. I guess what I'm saying is to indulge the fantasy in you much more. I mean, these are people whose fantasy life is not, I would say, normal! And I thought, Anna, that you went about Julie's inner life in kind of a normal way. There was no arbitrariness, there was no danger in your sense of just coming to him, or in your sense of sitting or in the sense of dancing.

And for you, Jeff — how much more interesting it would have been, for instance, if you had gotten up and really *shook* that woman! To the extent that you get furious and scare yourself with your own capacity for violence. And it becomes even scarier for you because, really, you are enjoying it! Or, at least, something in Jean enjoys it, so you better find that in yourself. If you indulge these things in yourself I think then you will see how the sexuality comes out as more than just flirtatiousness.

Do not worry about choices. Don't worry about interpretations. Because this is another play that is so brilliantly written, no matter what choice you make in the scene, somehow it's right. What we need to do, really, is stretch the opposites of what we're playing. Deal with the arbitrary and yet try to make that appear logical. Listen to your inner voices — let your blood interpret for you. Allow the sexuality to come out in one moment, allow the fear in another, allow neediness in another. Allowing all these random yet human things to come out in you, uncensored, is the most interesting thing you can do with material like this.

And don't choose when, where, and how to do them. That doesn't matter. Just connect with all those pieces of yourself, and let them come out, so that you scare each other. So that you scare yourselves, that you say: "Oh, God! I didn't know I had all that — ugliness or aggression or cruelty or lust or whatever — (*Nikos' voice rises, shaky with incredulity:*) I DID NOT KNOW THAT WAS IN ME!" Find what's dangerous in yourself in order to find the danger in the scene.

OBVIOUS CHOICES

The actors are working on the final scene between Valmont and Merteuil from Christopher Hampton's Les Liaisons Dangereuses, *based on the French novel by Choderlos de LaClos. Nikos starts by discussing how subtext emerges in relation to using words with specificity. He then talks about the pitfall of making obvious choices and obvious responses, and cautions the actors against the need to always register an immediate response to every line in the scene. The critique contains a technical lesson in using heightened language as well as Nikos' observations about the ways actors use their instruments to best (or worst) advantage.*

NIKOS: I'm sorry. I am going to stop it. (*Nikos has broken into the middle of the scene. His voice is forceful and quick, even angry.*) Look, just because the language is polite, whatever that is, it doesn't mean you make the decision that this is all about manners, that it is some kind of drawing room — it's wrong! You cannot act this scene unless you have some sense of the specificity of those words, that comes through because of the need, or because of the 'game-ness,' or whatever. You both were initially interesting to watch but you became so — unbelievably! — predictable that ultimately you were not only uninteresting, you were pedestrian!

Michelle, you go, (*Nikos speaks melodiously and very upper class, an English accent on top of the Greek:*) "Oh, I do this, and I do that and it's all in the sentences, and I can say that whole sentence very nicely." But that's about *sentences*. There are specific and subtextual *words* that you must select and chose to make the point clear. I mean, keep going, you'll see the great wealth of those lines.

ACTRESS: (*Playing Merteuil, continuing with the lines from the scene.*) "You loved that woman, Vicomte. What's more, you still do. Quite desperately. If you hadn't been so ashamed of it, how could you possibly have treated her so viciously? You can't bear —"

NIKOS: You see, again, "treat viciously." I mean, what are you really, specifically thinking about, what is your specific image when you say the word (*Whispered, like a hiss:*) "*viciously?*" It is not a cute line. Go ahead.

ACTRESS: "You can't bear even the vague possibility of being laughed at. And this has proved something I've always suspected. That vanity and happiness are incompatible."

NIKOS: You see, when you say "vanity and happiness," I don't know which is the important word. If you are accusing him with that word, if you are saying, "You are *vain*," then you say "*vanity* and happiness are incompatible." Then I know what it is about. Or, if you are saying that he is really making a search for his happiness, and "vanity and *happiness*" — which is what you want and desire — "are incompatible." But you can't say (*With equal weight:*) "vanity-and-happiness" like that because then we assume he has both, which is very wrong. Because it is not specific. Are you accusing him that he's vain? Or are you saying (*With great low strength:*) "In spite of all you are, you may not get your *happiness!*" If you say it that way, then *happiness* is the word you want him to remember when he leaves this room. Keep going.

ACTOR: (*Playing Valmont:*) "Whatever may or may not be the truth of these philosophical speculations —"

NIKOS: Okay. Now you're talking about "truth." If you hit the word "truth" then it might become that the two of you are truth-seekers. Or, that might not be the word. It might be "philosophical," these (*Sneeringly, emphasized:*) "*philosophical* speculations." They're not practical, they're not physical, they are *philosophical,* your speculations. What do you say next?

ACTOR: "The fact is it's now your turn to make a sacrifice."

NIKOS: Now if it is *your* turn, it means, as compared to mine. But if it is your *turn*, it relates to something else. And then, "to make a *sacrifice*" is something totally different.

So when you are going into that kind of language, which is brilliant, I think you have to be *so* damn specific about these things. What is amazing, I think, is that if you recorded the Royal Shakespeare Company performance of this play and just listened to it without being able to see it, you would still be able to get the whole thing. You find out that because of all the Shakespeare training, they use the words very differently than most American actors. And that's obviously why they had to bring in the whole company because we don't do that kind of work.

What you did was general. It was about these two people (*Casually:*) "Are you going to go to bed with me? I'm not going to go to bed with you." Nobody really cared. And even if the stakes get higher, it still wouldn't work because the stakes would still be general. It was not about *this* need in you or *that* need in you. And without that, you lose the specificity of who are those people are.

That is the difference between designing in broad strokes — I mean, in essence, if Jeremy Irons did that part the play would not have worked. Because he plays in broad strokes, he plays a whole quality rather than the very specific thing Alan Rickman does. It's a spectacular performance because it gets *so* specific. Now, what is fascinating is that specificity can change with each different actor — even from night to night. It is not that the specificity has to be about a certain thing. But, boy, by hitting certain words throughout, the subtext of the RSC production became so exciting, so fantastically alive.

Because you did not use words specifically, it shows your subtext was pedestrian. Because it was like (*Ho-hum:*) "Are you going to screw her or not?!" The words should be *more* loaded than even in a Pinter play, because it's even less specifically *stated* than some of the Pinter material, *The Homecoming* or *Betrayal* or something like that. And because this language is more extravagant. So there is even more subtext, and the subtext can go into a great many areas. Keep going through those lines and you'll see what I mean.

ACTOR: (*Valmont*) "Danceny must go."

ACTRESS: (*Merteuil*) " Where?"

ACTOR: "I've been more than patient about this little whim of yours, but enough is enough and I really must insist — "

NIKOS: Now again, I'm not sure if you should hit "little," or should we hear "whim?" Now you were right in hitting "I must" after that, but that is the more obvious thing, that is in terms of something the script calls for, so the *tone* hits her there. But in other places, it needs to be more than just the tone.

Now, besides not dealing with the specificity of the language, there was another problem which is why I stopped the scene. You are dying, Nina, to respond to the most immediate thing. And that gives you an ability to appear quick as an actress, but that stops you from dealing with something that might be more interesting, but it comes in a moment later. Beware of the most obvious response, and assume that you don't really have to respond right away. You don't really have to go (*Nikos makes different kinds of facial expressions and sounds:*) "Hum, ho, hah" right away. That's a problem with a lot of our acting, right? For example, a character says "I have come to pressure you." And the actor goes "Pressure, aha! Pressure is bad. That means I should register how badly I feel." Or somebody says "I have come to marry you." And the actor says "Oh, 'marry' is good so I better go — AHHH! — happy with that."

You know what I'm saying? Too many times we are taking the obvious words and giving the obvious responses, rather than having the "I'll wait-and-see" attitude — and then a little later I'll play. I don't know why. I guess somehow everybody assumes that they are always on the spot on the stage. Actors think that the whole world doesn't watch the person who talks, but watches all over the stage. Unlike a symphony where you see a lot of the instruments not playing, right? Actors don't want to do that on stage. They want to respond with the most obvious thing. And "life" to most actors doesn't mean *life*, it means some kind of *activity*. Because you can have life and be neutral. You can have life and not respond to anything until you hear the word that triggers your response. The way, as I said, an orchestra does. Somebody holds here, somebody turns the page, somebody doesn't always have to hit a note to answer the other instruments. Somebody holds something — (*Nikos takes a pause, then sings:*) "Dum dum" — and then he plays. Which is great.

But on stage because people are watching, actors feel they should always have an attitude of approval or disapproval to what the other person says, rather than a wait-and-see attitude. Again when you watch really wonderful acting, someone can actually be on that stage and you don't even know that they're there! But for the most part, everybody's very eager, you know, to act! Rather than saying, "When somebody throws the ball at me, I'll throw it back. And before that, I'm just kind of looking to find out where the ball is." And this is what was happening to you in the scene. When the other person spoke you constantly had a need to have something, an attitude. So the attitude many times was not specific, it came in a general way, it came in prefabricated, rather than saying to yourself, "I'm an unwritten blackboard."

So, I suggest that you just — rethink everything. Throw it all away, what you did today, take a blank slate and begin again.

PREMEDITATED ACTING

Having directed a dozen productions of Chekhov's plays at the Williamstown Theatre Festival, Nikos approaches this playwright with a special expertise. The scene in question between Yelena and Astrov is from the third act of Uncle Vanya. *Nikos talks here about the problem of making choices that "underline" the text, resulting in behavior that is "symbolic" rather than organic. He encourages the actors not to "choreograph" their behavior, but to let it spring from the circumstances in the scene.*

NIKOS: I wish you [*Astrov*] were as carried away by the maps as you were carried away by the love for her. Think of *Candida,* when someone recites poetry to the person they love, or paints a picture for the person they love. Astrov's speech about the maps becomes the way he expresses love instead of saying, 'I love you.' It's not really avoidance, it's not really a substitution, it is a direct way of dealing energetically with loving her. It's the way great singers like Frank Sinatra sing — it becomes a kind of lovemaking through another medium. And I felt that would've given you something to hold onto, even though I felt your authority and simplicity was really so much better.

Now, [*Astrov*] you have the line to her at the end of the speech: "You're not paying attention." You could've said this to her two or three times, and much, much earlier than Chekhov gives you the line! Because obviously she was going out of her way to tell us that she was not paying attention! [*Yelena*], you became a walking stage direction to justify his eventual line about your lack of interest in his maps. You don't have to be that obvious. And [*Astrov*], what I lost somehow was the sense that you are waiting for her to eventually get involved with this subject that you care about so much.

It's interesting how you both were not helping yourselves physically, by sitting back in the chairs. How much more interesting it would've been, when you say, [*Yelena*], "Now we have to talk," if you'd taken him to the couch because you really do want to talk rather than making it an interrogation. So that there would be an accessibility and an availability to it. You were leaning back, [*Astrov*] rather than leaning almost forward and saying, (*With eagerness:*) "Yeah," "Uh-huh," "Yes!" So from your physicality, I thought you both were holding yourself back from dealing with the sort of things that control you, that overtake you. When the love came out all of a sudden, the grabbing and trying to kiss was interesting, but it was not as necessary as it should have been. As it would have been if you hadn't been so suspicious of each other.

There was such a cleanness to the scene in the beginning that was fascinating. But then you both really started getting very scared of the scene and going back to certain kinds of tricks you do. The tricks you do are really very peculiar because, for example, [*Yelena*], you gave yourself the freedom in the monologue at very beginning to do whatever you wanted to do with the speech. And yet you felt compelled to pick up the scarf that kept falling! So the fact that you have to maintain the scarf around your neck closes you in. You seem to have decided to lie across the table, but because that is very difficult acrobatically, it becomes choreographed, it becomes like a number. I mean, if you have to make decisions, don't decide *what* you're going to do, decide *why* you're going to do it. Decide to feel like running around, don't decide how you're going to run around, just run around! Roll all over the bed, jump up and down, decide things that would help your acting rather than things that tell us what your acting is. You block yourself emotionally that way, you were hurting yourself. You did all these things that were symbolic of freedom, rather than being the sort of things that come out of giving yourself permission, as an actress, to actually to free yourself.

Now, you established four to five times, you made it clear that you were not interested in his maps. That is not what she would do! What she would certainly do is *try* to be interested and find out she's not interested. That is the acting task. The acting task is not for you to justify for us his line "Oh, I can see you're not interested." It is justified. Since you knew that line was coming up, you were trying from the very beginning to justify it. The fact that he can see that you are not interested doesn't mean that we should all should see it and should see it so far in advance, because then it becomes ludicrous!

Same thing with the chair, [*Yelena*]. You sat down to talk to him, and yet you kept turning your head away from him and not looking at him, you dealt with the idea of indignation rather than "Don't come closer to me!" Now, when someone says "Don't come closer to me," they don't go and sit the way you did on that sofa! It was kind of coy — and also it's theatrical. You associate the business you come up with on stage with a certain theatrical elegance, with theatrical gestures, and that's not why people do business on stage. You do business up on the stage to make you feel closer to the kind of feeling you want to have when you're really living the scene. You kept contradicting yourself in the scene because you dealt with freedom, and then you would give yourself tasks that required regimentation. You dealt with danger, yet your behavior was theatrical, not frightening. You didn't go against a wall, you did not start backing up from him, you didn't allow this scene to be dangerous for yourself.

I guess I wish, [*Yelena*], at the beginning, that you would allow the speech to happen while you're talking. I mean, you are upset about Sonya, and you are worrying about your own life. Now, you were dealing many times with what you were *realizing* in the speech rather than what you were *trying to find out*. And when you realize something and then state it emotionally or verbally, you're in trouble because then the words become idle. The words become idle because you're not trying to actually find something out with the text. When you were walking up and down it helped because —

ACTRESS: That was the only part of that monologue that I felt comfortable with because it was the only thing that sort of came…

NIKOS: That is because you gave yourself a chance to walk with no purpose, which gave you a feeling of: 'I'm trying to find out what it's all about.' But the rest of it — you were like a text that is underlined. When you said the part about being a mermaid, you did something with your feet, and then you went to the table on the next line, but that was a kind of difficult thing to do, it really was. You turned away in a very peculiar way, you were doing a lot things that were like, mildly theatrical, and I think you have to watch that. I thought the simplicity improved, but you're doing things that say you want us to know that you understand something about the script, rather than dealing with the openness of the text which is — (*Loosely, inarticulately.*) "I'd like to ask you something, I don't know how I'm going to ask it, it doesn't really matter, I'm just going to ask something." And then, you'll see, it becomes far more involving for you.

If we had a film of what you just did, you'd find out that you really love to do things when somebody else is talking. You know? Every time [Astrov] was doing anything you were registering little opinions: "Yes." "No." "Maybe." "This is what I feel about this." "This is what I feel about that." So it as if you distrust the life of the scene. Because let me tell you, nobody's going to look at you at that particular moment, you know? Or if they look at you they should really be thinking of him anyway, which means that listening is an extremely important part of your work. You seem to be programmed to be acting in your own way, independent of him. And I thought that because of that, you were eager to register your reaction to things before he even did them.

I think once again, what we saw here today was just too much acting! A lot of acting. Divide it into blocks, divide it into units, divide it into chapters rather than into words. I thought it was good that your voice sounded much more real than I have heard it, and certain moments in the scene showed your progress as an actress. But in between you put in little things, little acting doodles, so I got lost. When actors put in little sounds in between the words, you know, sounds of laughter, sounds of tears, or even little words like "huh" or "um," you just say, "What's going on?" Because these little, parenthetical bits of acting are going on all over the place, we lose what's going on in the scene.

Be less reverent. Kind of try to say to yourself, "Oh, it's really not that great being up there and the sooner I do it the better I feel." I mean, you're just very reluctant to stop acting, so you act all sorts of things between the acting that the playwright gives you.

ACTRESS: When I first started to work on the monologue, I worked strictly on the emotional content of it — and then it was very bland. I mean, not bland, it was emotional, but then I also wanted to do certain business, so I felt like I also had to direct it. I tried to direct it and then stand back and get to the emotion…

NIKOS: I'm not sure why you do that. You could have done business or not done business but the speech is not going to make it because of that! I guess what I'm saying is that if you're going to put in business, put in business that helps your feeling rather than that demonstrates your ability to understand the text. Do less. You really do two to three things in every moment rather than just one, and that hurts you. Do it more directly, deal with it more openly.

[*Astrov*], for you too, it would have been good if you'd found, physically, some position when you go to her, you know, throwing yourself on the couch, or on your knees, it would be great to find some ways to help you physically define the objective. And I suggest that you have the maps in three different places so it's not so regimented, so that you can move the speech with more freedom.

And, please — I know once again I repeat myself, but try not to set things. We all need to go to our junkyards and come back with three thousand things, try them out, to find out what works. If you come to rehearsals with your five set ideas, you're sunk. You can't re-create the world of the play according to what you already know, only according to what you're discovering.

COMMENTARY
BY LYNNE MEADOW

> *Lynne Meadow has been the Artistic Director of the Manhattan Theatre Club (MTC) since 1972. There, she has produced and directed over 100 New York and world premieres and under her guidance MTC productions have garnered six Tony Awards, two Pulitzer Prizes, thirty Obie Awards, and thirteen Drama Desk Awards as well as the 1987 Lucille Lortel Award for Outstanding Achievement. A graduate of Bryn Mawr, Ms. Meadow also attended Yale School of Drama and has taught at Circle in the Square Theatre School, Yale University, and NYU.*

As I read these transcripts of Nikos' acting classes, I am flooded with glorious memories of this extraordinary man — memories of how thrilling it was to be in one of his classes. Reading his words, I am struck over and over — just as I was at age twenty-one when I first met him — by the gigantic talent he had as a teacher and as a mentor; he was really one of the most brilliant and articulate masters of the theater I have ever known. We used to joke as students that Nikos' Greek accent got more pronounced every year: We knew that wasn't really true but somehow we must have been feeling intimidated by this man's unique ability to explain, to use words in what was his second language. He spoke in ways none of us had ever heard, or that frankly I would ever hear again.

Nikos had an uncanny ability to "diagnose" a theatrical event. In what always seemed like record time, he could describe the essence of a character, the essence of a scene, or the essence of an entire play for that matter. He was one of those people who was totally connected to his instincts and reactions; he was also blessed with a prodigious intelligence. And the combination of his instincts and his intelligence made him a giant force of *sheer perception.*

There are so many Nikos-isms in these pages, like "You must never allow the form of the material to stop the life of the material." He had this way of criticizing work so accurately that a student's reaction was inevitably, "Of course. Why didn't I think of that? — it seems so obvious." Nikos' brilliance was exactly that he could illuminate the obvious; he could explain the basics; he could get to the heart of the matter, but he always made his students probe themselves to find their own truths. One of the millions of things I admired about him was how nurturing he was, how utterly supportive of his students. He never pretended there was only one way to create art — he wanted you to find your own vision, to tap into yourself (he certainly refers to this over and over in these critiques) and to find, as he told his directing students, your own unique signature. "You know it's a Picasso just by looking. So too you as directors must find your own signature." Nikos was an Art History major at Oberlin, and so often his references were to painting or painters.

Nikos was ruthless about finding the inner logic of a scene — but paradoxically he used logic only as a means to unlock spontaneity. He always exhorted his students to discard the "intellectual" and to find the root, the primal, the psychological, the personal, the very essence of your own humanity.

I first met Nikos in 1968 when I was one of six directing students at the Yale School of Drama. He taught a famous course called Drama 10 for Directors, which was attended by designers and dramaturgs as well. It was a scene study class, and the word was to be wary of directing your three- to five-minute scene from either Chekhov or Williams since Nikos was so gifted with these playwrights.

I can remember directing my first scene for him as if it were yesterday — I chose the lawyer scene from Arthur Miller's *A View From the Bridge,* a scene in which Eddie Carbone implores Alfieri to help him. I dissected every word with my two actors, figured out every beat, and created what I thought was damn good work. After the presentation, Nikos walked onstage and moved Eddie's chair just far enough away so that the actor could not touch the lawyer Alfieri's desk. He then asked the actors to redo the scene. Suddenly there was greater tension, a greater sense of frustration, a feeling of powerlessness for the actor playing Eddie. And I marveled as this wise Socratic soul showed me how much it means for a director to create an appropriate obstacle for an actor to overcome in a scene. "What did you see?" he would always ask. He was a constant champion of getting his students to watch — not to think about what you saw but to "experience" it. He was full of gems of advice — I remember his telling us directors that sometimes we would ask the actors to do a run-through just to reassure ourselves that all was proceeding well — "There's no point," he'd say, "in trying to make a pearl necklace until you have all the pearls." *Do the work* was his message. Probe, discover, play, delve, investigate. And then throw it all away and just be.

I was the only woman in my class at Yale; in fact, in my second year I was the only woman directing student in the school. I was nervous about that and wondered if I would be treated equally. But Nikos early on certainly singled me out as one of his favorites, which was an enormous source of pride to me. After my first year at Yale, Nikos asked me to be his assistant at Williamstown where I spent two summers, and I'm sure my work as an Artistic Director of a major theatre — as well as my work as a director — was totally shaped by my time with Nikos. Over the years I was always in touch with him; I was always the beneficiary of his brilliant advice. This is a man who had a profound influence on who I am. I will always be indebted to him for all that he gave me and I will always love him and his extraordinary spirit.

PART THREE
"Drop by Drop, Knowledge Comes to the Unwilling"

I love actors. I love them because they're brave. All good work requires self-revelation. A musician communicates feelings through the instrument he is playing, a dancer through body movement. The talent of acting is one in which the actor's thoughts and feelings are instantly communicated to the audience. In other words, the "Instrument" that an actor is using is himself. It is his feelings, his physiognomy, his sexuality, his tears, his laughter, his anger, his romanticism, his tenderness, his viciousness, that are up there on the screen for all to see. That's not easy. In fact, quite often it's painful.

Sidney Lumet
Making Movies

ACTING WITHOUT PURPOSE

In this scene between Lorna and Joe from Golden Boy *by Clifford Odets, Nikos again urges the actors to transcend the superficial traits of the characters to find the more hidden, primitive needs. It is for the audience, he suggests, to come up with the reasons why characters say and do things in a certain way, not for the actors to lead the audience by the hand with their acting.*

NIKOS: I wish you knew less about who these characters are. I wish the scene was not so accessible — that the relationship was not so possible from the very beginning. It's fascinating writing because these people are really nothing except puppets of certain forces. If they could talk together easily, the way you did now, there would be no problem. I kept saying to myself "Let's just cut to the chase and let them say to each other (*As the characters, quickly and easily:*) "So it's you and me, kid," "Right?" "Right." "Okay?" "Okay." There was not the peculiar miracle of a — cripple getting together with a blind person. The scene feeds in terms of two people who really don't belong together getting together. It's about the romance and naiveté of Odets — these two people get together — and then at the end of it they drive off to get killed.

Someone commented after the scene that the story was told clearly. I think it's more than the story being told clearly. When I saw the two of you, if it weren't for the costume I would not know there was a kind of a difference between these two people, that Odets is dealing with something dangerous, with dark, peculiar ingredients of a certain kind of human soul. Because the scene was so accessible for both of them, the language and the words surprised me. If these people understood each other so well, they would not be using those words, they would be doing something else.

Connie, you are fascinating up there but you just do it like the stage directions. You really do the chewing gum and the thing with the hair to tell me what the character is all about. I just wish there was this feeling of (*Lost, at large:*) "Who am I, I don't know! I might be this and I might be that but I don't know who I am because I never had time to examine myself!" It's the same thing I told you about your work in *The Rainmaker*. It's not "underneath-it-all-I'm-interested-in-you-and-I-pretend-not-to-be." But it's that she doesn't even *know* that she's interested. I recently looked at the tape of Barbara Stanwyck playing Lorna, and it's amazing because you don't know that there's any love there in this scene and she does not know either up till the last moment, when a kind of naiveté escapes.

We all interpret too much. By interpreting too much we are taking the audience's hand and telling them what they should think about the scene, rather than assuming that the result of the scene is revealed because there are primitive needs and primitive desires and passions between the characters. Your acting is persuasive, Connie, but allow yourself to move in directions that you have not counted on. Move to things that are really secret and make everybody say "What is she doing?" rather than feeling so obligated to show us. I wish I had seen the fact that she avoids being in love with him, the fact that she fights against it. And with you, Jamie, it's not all so sweet. It's not (*Romantically:*) "I love you," it's (*Angrily:*) "I love you, goddamn it!" It would be much easier for him not to love her, wouldn't it?

I just thought you made it into a nice scene rather than a dangerous scene. It's a problematic scene anyway, this second scene on the bench, it's a toughie. But what is interesting, I think, is for us to look at the two of you and say: "Oh, I wish the other side of their nature would come out." The part of their nature that matches in those two people in spite of what they are saying, and in spite of what they are really doing. And because they don't use that part of their nature very much, when they do, they don't do it very well. It's almost like trying to touch and missing. So then when these two people get finally get together, you as the actor, you as the character, are surprised. Rather than knowing all along the inevitability of that kiss. If you had really worked much more on the acting for no purpose, you'd find that the scene would move in peculiar ways, that these two people get together against all logic and against all possibility, and then the kiss would be such a big surprise. And if it's a surprise, you'd find that everybody would applaud because then it would have that — Wow! — that sense of coming out in a completely unprotected, unexpected way.

Because if you are not surprised by your own acting, then you do not make a good moment also a frightening moment or a dangerous moment, or whatever. You played it safe. You know, it is a naive scene. There is a great deal of primitiveness. So that no matter what people try to be, their nature speaks for them.

I'm just not sure that when people psychoanalyze themselves, the way that Connie's character does in the scene, that they are doing it accurately — with the proper emphasis and the proper way of dealing with it. If somebody says (*Loudly, off the cuff:*) "Well, I've acted a lot and I've directed a lot and I know a lot about theater," I'm not really sure they know that they are dealing with bravado. They think they are dealing with something else. I'm not sure that when these characters speak that they *know* how much harshness there is in what they're saying. It's the same thing as saying (*Plaintively:*) "I hurt" in order to get sympathy, which really doesn't work because then it becomes manipulative. Rather than saying, (*Simply, without pity:*) "I hurt, and then I go on, I do this and that…" I think that's why I keep talking always about Chekhov, how fascinating he is, because he never makes his characters tell you how they feel. You know? He makes people do certain kinds of actions. Let the audience add it up. Let them say: "I think she does it because of that." Because those things are very hidden within people anyway. It is for somebody else to say: "I see a lot of anger there, I see a lot of frustration there." Or "I see a lot of protection there." The audience should see these things in all different ways depending on their own associations.

I mean, sometimes I have a problem with a person and a friend will say to me, "Don't you realize he's doing that because he feels insecure?" I say, "Of course I don't realize it, because that person tells me things to make it very clear how secure he is." And it kind of always fascinates me when people in the non-theater world see a play I've directed, and come up with a diagnosis and a meaning that is so different from what I really see up there theatrically! It's fascinating.

When I first met Lee Strasberg, I thought he was the rudest man ever, because he wouldn't look at me. When I first started, there was a party at the Strasberg's every year and they used to invite everybody, like, two thousand people, I don't know! And you get a card saying "The Strasbergs invite you," and you feel very good that the Strasbergs invite you! So I go there and his wife Anna turns to him and says, "Lee this is Nikos." At which point he looks at me and says (*Loud, gruff:*) "SO?"

So I stood there and I said (*Nervously:*) "Uh, hi, I am Nikos." He walked away! And from then on, that was it! I couldn't even talk to the guy. And then five years later I met his daughter and told her about meeting her father, and Susan said "Well that's because he knows a lot about you and he really likes you and he was very, very happy to meet you." It's amazing! And then I started going to the studio a lot, I got to know him, and I realized in effect he was a very shy guy, and because of that he just manifests as — and he didn't know! He just thought that was like, a nice, personal, private greeting — (*Sharply:*) "SO?" AAAAAHHH! (*Nikos makes a characteristic sound that expresses both pleasure and a need to cut the laughter from the students and move on.*)

So. I'm just saying, I don't think people always know what their behavior spells and once you are making a point as an actor that you know, you are minimizing the importance of the secret, animal things that are longing to come out of the character, and out of yourself.

AGAINST INTERPRETATION

The two actresses here are working on a scene from David Rabe's In the Boom Boom Room, *but Nikos remarks are not specifically textual. In this critique he deals with the kind of process the actor needs to cultivate for work in any scene, so that the acting becomes "empirical" (relying or based on experiment and observation) — rather than cerebral (work based on a thought process involving interpretation and judgement.)*

NIKOS: You know the great line George has at the end of that big scene in *Our Town?* He says, "Emily, I guess we've had a very important conversation." But all through the scene they didn't know it! They didn't really know till the end of the scene that they had an important conversation. And I think in all our work, that is what's essential.

I thought both of you were very moving. I think this was your best scene ever, Jesse. I thought the moments when you were trying to smile and the times you were lost and had not a clue — that was great. But, first, there was such a decision from both of you to deal with who these people are as characters. Somebody in the class remarked that the great contrast between the two of you was terrific. But I wish there was not that much of a contrast. You took the differences between the two women, which theoretically appear in the script, and made them so pronounced that your entire acting was based on that. As I keep saying, when you make characters so pronounced you lose the potential for dimension. The potential for one person in the audience to say, "Oh, she is naive," and another person to say "No she's not naive, she's frightened." When you do character in such a way that everybody can speculate, that is the time you know the acting makes sense, because then you are not following a program.

I think both of you were following programs. When you follow programs it might make you feel safer, but it creates a distance between you and the character. For example, Marsha, you turned out and did the long speech in a very romantic way. You were summoning it in your imagination and talking about this imaginary scenario in a way that really has nothing to do with acting. You were really performing that particular speech, not acting it. The greatest monologues are moments when the sense of privacy becomes public. That's, really, something that was so apparent with Blythe Danner in *Three Sisters,* in that monologue where Masha confesses her love for Vershinin. That what all great actors do is make their private worlds public, and that's the difference between a good actor and a bad actor. That's all it is — giving themselves permission to appear to be silly and ridiculous and emotional and human and glorious.

The speech did not come out of a peculiar need, which is what acting is. A need that you do not completely understand, which makes the acting subconscious — and therefore more interesting: because you are acting in spite of yourself rather than because of yourself. Marsha, you *love* to act because of yourself. When someone says "sit," you sit. If you say "Let me talk to you," it is about exactly that. It's not (*Letting loose, chaotically:*) "I want to talk to you, I'm upset, I'm annoyed, let me interrupt you." No, when you say, "Let me talk to you," you mean (*Measured, pedantic:*) "Let-me-talk-to-you." When you did that big speech about that boy, it became a romantic moment. Instead of out of a need. (*Nikos paraphrases the speech, speaking loosely, inarticulately, without hesitancy.*) "You know what happened to me? I — I like men, I have no problem with men, but there was one guy, one guy, you know, that treated me, well, bad, and ever since — that time, I look at them differently, that's all, I look at them differently!" So that you don't even know what saying the speech means! So that at the end you surprise yourself! And then not just the audience, but even you speculate about *why* you made such a speech.

Marsha, you are dying to score points in terms of knowing what you are doing up there. Now, you're very bright. You read the play and you interpret it. But when you are acting, your task is to find elements of the material which take you totally away from what you know, that connect to a hidden element of yourself. If you hook up with that hidden element in yourself that is specific to the material, and if that hidden element really disturbs you and really throws you off, then you gain dimension. Then everyone who is watching you will have a different take on why you are doing what you're doing. Most of the time people do not know why they are saying things that they say. And on stage they should not, either. They should know in the rehearsal, they should know when they analyze the script but they should not know when they get up there. Why? When actors "don't know" onstage, it allows all sorts of other interesting, unconscious things to come forward and play.

Here, the scene was about a conversation, it was not about peculiar feelings that are expressed in an inarticulate way. Just like many people in life, these two characters are not articulate but they think they are articulate. You seemed to think your task was to demonstrate certain character traits in these women, such as harshness or innocence. No. Your task is to connect certain needs of your own with the material, which then allows the more secret things come out. I keep wondering what are the secret things that you'd be caught off-guard doing up on that stage.

ACTRESS: I was caught I guess, because I saw that speech as part of my end of the discussion. That the speech is there because —

NIKOS: I just wish you wouldn't see so many things as things!

ACTRESS: Okay. — What?

NIKOS: I wish you would not make judgements like that! I wish you would assume that if you're doing certain tasks onstage something else will come out that is very interesting. That's exactly what I'm telling you. I'm telling you that you are *seeing* things as this and that, and you are planning this and that, so that what comes out is a program of decisions that you have made. Rather than, here we are doing certain tasks, having our lives. We are changing clothes, we're setting up the food, we're getting ready to go out and in between we have a conversation. I mean, come on, when people approach you in the street and start talking, you think to yourself, "Uh oh! That person subconsciously probably wants to do this or do that." It's not as if the person knows what he's saying, it is in his nature. But you seem to always know what you're doing, and then making certain kind of choices to support that knowledge —

ACTRESS: I think I know what you mean.

NIKOS: — then, what happens is that you are not alive. I think you'll find out that most interesting acting really happens when it's been plotted way back, so in a way it's been forgotten. I'm always fascinated when I interview people for the first time, I'm fascinated by why somebody talks so much or why someone adjusts their chair, and you think: "How many times is that person going to adjust their chair?" And because the circumstances are totally new, that is when you can really tell things about character, even things that people don't want you to know, or that they don't even know about themselves.

Your strong moments were very interesting, Marsha, which shows me that you should use your strength more, rather than using your tendency to turn speeches into, really, arias. Your big speeches in the scene were kind of theatrical things.

ACTRESS: Did you see it like that, like an aria, or it shouldn't be that?

NIKOS: It shouldn't be that.

ACTRESS: See, I thought that was what I should do! Because it's so weird, because the playwright has the lighting change when she goes into the speeches and—

NIKOS: But you know, this play was done three times and every time unsuccessfully. We did the original version up in Williamstown, we took off forty-five minutes and it seemed equally long! Then Joe Papp brought it back and took off another forty-five minutes, and it never, ever seemed shorter! And that's because the playwright is really hung up on certain kind of things. But you can't really assume if you're given a stage direction, that it is right!

ACTRESS: No, I know that, but—

NIKOS: Shakespeare says, "Enters" and "Exits." And that's all you really need. And even Chekhov, who writes some directions, usually only suggests a pause. And that pause can mean anything. It's not a specific take on a moment.

And sure, somebody who is dying all his life to be theatrical, all of a sudden takes a moment like that and isolates it with light. But it's really a very stupid speech, isn't it? Unless she has a strong emotional reason for saying it, there's no point. The speech is a sense memory, in the terms of the way a character might say, "I went to this place and I ate this food." And then later on says, "I went somewhere else and ate that food." And in the audience you say, "Aha!, that guy really likes his food." But let the audience draw that conclusion, if as an actor you know this conclusion ahead of time you are really hurting it.

I wonder, really, why actors do this. Let me put it this way, I've worked with hundreds of people and it's just amazing how many people do that: think ahead to what the result should be. Again I go back to someone I like very much — Joanne Woodward — and she wants to talk about all these things. She says, "I think I should play it this way, I think I should play it that way, because the character does this and that." And I just say: "Forget it, I don't want to know anything about that. I just want you to touch this. Or here, you drink. Don't worry about why you drink. If you drink five times and you drink fast, something is going to come out of that."

It is never, "This character is this, and that character is that." Because then, rather than allowing the enjoyment that comes on stage by finding things and bouncing off everyone else, you become determined to pick up *only* this and *only* that. So you *arrive* someplace but you do not *travel* on stage. You lose the ability to be open to seeing other things.

That's why, you see, I'm so much against interpretation. That's why I love rehearsing plays upside down. This moment here, that moment there, a little scene from Act Three, a little scene from Act Two, a little scene from Act One. All out of sequence. Find the moments rather than how they add up. Don't assume that the work is all in the sequence, in the order, in the clarity, in the point of view. A lot of it is in the life, and in order to cultivate life on the stage, you have to do certain things that *allow* other things to come out. I think it's essential — and easier! — to allow things to come out rather than deciding "I want to get to this and this" and then going ahead and doing just that. So many times when I watch acting I keep watching choices rather than the cultivation of another world. Make the circumstances vivid for yourself, make your own personal response and your own emotional world connect with the world the playwright gives you and then *see* what comes out. That's much more interesting. That's why I think, Jesse, those moments when you were smiling really worked. Because when you were smiling it was the most helpless thing ever. You were not smiling because you were happy, you were smiling because you were lost, and that's when the helplessness came out.

But also, you needed to find the situation. Then it would have been wonderful. If you find the situation, if you try to cook or arrange furniture, whatever, it would be so great for the two of you. If you get involved with some physical tasks, it makes it easier for lines to come out without thinking. If you had found the life, then your acting would have just come out without you knowing how it was coming out. Now you made it a conversation, and when you have time to have a conversation you have to pass judgement and when you have time to pass judgement you are in trouble with material like that.

ACTRESS: We had staged the whole cracker and wine thing, but somehow it —

NIKOS: — got lost. Yeah. Because you were interested in talking. But when people just sit and talk, they talk programmatically, trying to make certain points, right? I don't know why people talk anyway, I mean, they try to transcend something else, I guess. There is this whole thing now about (*Dismissively:*) "Let's talk!" I guess they can't do other things well, so they talk! But when people do that, they really plan to say certain things to get certain things. So it becomes a conversation about two points of view. Which is really not as interesting as the points of view appearing through the situation. You see, I didn't know who is hot or who is cold, I didn't know who has all the time, and who doesn't, who is wearing something tight and should be changing, who is hungry, who is tired. I didn't know anything about any of the things that give texture and life and also makes it more interesting for you to play, when it's less programmatic.

Again, it's the old Stanislavski thing, cultivate the dirt and don't worry about the flowers, the flowers will bloom. Cultivate the dirt. Get the circumstances going, get all of the stuff that surrounds the scene and then something results that's more interesting. Rather than dealing with the guideposts. Rather than dealing with, moment "A" we get this and moment "B" we do that and moment "C" is about that. Because then it's not a — journey. When you travel in a scene, sometimes you see this, sometimes you see that. You grab at this, and you don't have enough time to jump for that, somebody else jumps you. It is empirical, not cerebral.

TOUCHING BASE

> *In commenting on this scene from Chekhov's* Ivanov *(between the title character and Sasha, the young girl who loves him) Nikos describes the importance of moment-to-moment work having a foundation in a consistent need the character has, supported by the circumstances of the script — rather than on arbitrary choices made by the actor. He talks about the actor discovering in the part and in himself the underlying need of the character that repeatedly feeds every line and every choice the actor makes. Without that need, Nikos suggests the work becomes "graffiti" and lacks ease and inevitability.*

NIKOS: I think the whole problem, because of the specificity of a play like an *Ivanov,* is that your moment-to-moment work didn't make sense. You both did not go back between moments to your original impulse, your original need, and then start from there all over again. So the different things you did were almost denying each other.

For example, [*Ivanov*], you decided for no apparent reason to clear the table, to deal with the bread crumbs, but there was so much that you were doing that did not connect you with something that the material is saying about him being a failure. He says "I'm a kind of failure, I no longer feel anything." You didn't use that as the character's emotional center and your own emotional center as the blocks that everything else builds from.

[*Sasha*], sometimes you went toward him and dealt with love, and sometimes you dealt with understanding, and sometimes you dealt with him with annoyance, and sometimes you dealt with trying to manufacture a certain amount of energy with him. But there was really no emotional point of view. There was no possibility for inevitability in your acting because you had not decided that she has come in to woo him, let's say, or take him away from his wife or to seduce him, or whatever. Whatever was hitting you, you were doing! So it was very interesting and very alive, but it was like doing two steps forward and one step back, three to the right, two to the left, etcetera.

The same thing with you, [*Ivanov*]. Basically you were not dealing with Ivanov as a man who wants desperately to feel certain things but he doesn't really feel anything. (*Nikos acts out the following as he speaks.*) He is upset and he meanders and he drinks the wine in a certain way, the same way that he opens the book, the same way that he moves away from her, the same way that he goes and opens the windows — and by "the same way," I mean behavior that is always based on a certain, similar kind of need. Instead of having that need which informs everything you do, you on the other hand were — indiscriminate! Sometimes you were very active, sometimes you were very lethargic, you were leaving her to go and drink wine, you were going to break the bottle capriciously rather than saying (*Frustrated, upset:*) "Okay, because you tell me to break something I will try to break it, I will try to break it! (*Resigned:*) — No I better not break it, leave me alone, I can't even get up from my chair — (*Elongated, loud:*) — PLEASE!"

Now, because every moment was so different from every other moment, you were not allowing the acting instrument to pile up each piece of information and make some kind of sense. Touch base. If you feel that the material is as colorful as that, touch base between lines. Touch base back to the main things that make you do the scene, with the main thread that is there. It is not that you obliterate the differences in the scene, but it's that they all are fed through the same kind of source.

You see, [*Sasha*], when you kept going and kneeling to him it seemed interesting, but when you knelt you only dealt with the love. You have to filter that love through the lack of patience that you have as well, your impatience with somebody like him. The same thing with you, [*Ivanov*]. There is no reason for you, every time you say one thing to her, to forget the fact that your other lines are "There is nothing I can do, please leave me alone." When you have a line like "This is the dog, it's painted from memory," it's not exclusively about how the picture was painted, you know! It's you [*Sasha*], in your frustration, wanting to get back to the so-called "real" world. Everything you pick up, everything you do comes out of the same needs which in the end, spells something. In the scene I just saw, you, [*Sasha*], became Ivanov many times, and you [*Ivanov*] became Sasha. I did not know who was who! I did not know who was dragging and who was being dragged, I did not know who was pushing and who was being pushed.

Look at the circumstances of the material. She keeps trying to make you change, right? That presupposes that there is something sick about you, right? Now, it doesn't matter how you interpret it, you might interpret it that you're just a very lethargic person, you might interpret it that you're so confused and so messed up, but she's the one who keeps saying "Come on, do it, change!" But obviously in listening to all these lines, it should give you a clue of the character's emotional impotence, and because of that, a clue about the way the character has of dealing with life. But you kept changing, both of you, not because the playwright gave you a way to change, and not because your partner was changing. One didn't relate to the other. There were all these interesting things you were doing, but it was graffiti time for both of you rather than designing time or planning time. I suggest that you think of the scene as much less horizontal — and much more vertical in terms of — (*Nikos acts it out, vocally building one thing on top of another.*) "I'm going to deal with the fact that I'm so upset, and so concerned and I just don't have the energy to be dealing with that woman!"

So, I think that moment-to-moment acting in a scene does not necessarily mean that each moment has to be so different from the others, it means that the *adaptations* are different, but the center of the material is the same. If you find the center of your acting, the acting becomes easy and inevitable, and then of course, it *appears* inevitable which is great, which is what we all want. And the acting also appears accidental. But if you do not find that point of view, that center, then it's almost like everything that comes into the scene grabs you in a different way — not further on the road toward whatever the scene is going, but as a distraction. You were both very distracted in terms of what you were dealing with in the scene, because I think that you did not have a strong point of reference in terms of the needs of your characters.

In Greece, you know, people bring pine cones to weddings — why I don't know! But there's an expression, "Don't leave the wedding to look for the pine cones." You know? I mean, Chekhov says it, it's the doctor's line from *The Sea Gull*. About not going down the picturesque road.* You have to do moment-to moment acting in Chekhov, but it's not *picturesque* moment-to-moment. It's moment-to-moment that is informed by a consistent emotional need.

---

*Dorn, in Act I of The Sea Gull *says:* "In a work of art there must be a clear, definite idea. You must know what your object is in writing, for if you follow that picturesque road without a definite aim, you will go astray and your talent will be your ruin."

MALADJUSTED ACTING

> *In his critique of a scene from Shelagh Delaney's* A Taste of Honey, *because essential acting ingredients are still missing, Nikos does not deal with the resulting "stew" but the missing ingredients themselves. In stressing the importance of "making efforts," Nikos suggests techniques for uncovering the actor's temperament and cultivating "maladjustment" in both the work and the character.*

NIKOS: I think as you go about working a scene you should think of all the unspoken things rather than the spoken. The scene suffered to a great extent because you created such an ease in reaching each other. I keep saying that theater is not about adjustment, it's about *mal*adjustment. And obviously the characters in this particular play have a great deal of mal adjustment. But because you made them people without problems you can't really have a scene. You both seemed without problems because nothing seemed to come out of peculiar, neurotic needs you might have.

Even if we don't stick to the interpretation, the circumstances tell us that he is alone, he's homosexual, he does not have a place to stay and that she treats him very peculiarly, so it's a very weird relationship. And at the end of it there are lines something like, "We're both degenerates — we're both beggars," but there was certainly nothing beggarly or degenerate in either of you.

Somehow, the things you're saying have to be contrary, or diametrically opposed to some other things that are rooted inside you. It has to be not necessarily opposite but contrasting to what appears, and that is how you make efforts. You did not make an effort to do the scene. Efforts are made because one person hates and the other loves, or because both people cannot — this scene is so clear — both people cannot adjust to reality. There was a sense that both of you wanted to do *exactly* what you were doing with the scene. That makes for great social reality, but not very interesting behavioral reality, where in effect the subconscious needs, the dark needs, come into the body. You cannot have that unless you carry within you an imaginary text with circumstances different from the circumstantial evidence of the play.

Howard, there was a moment in the scene when you stepped on something, and it obviously was not something you rehearsed. I thought it would've been fascinating for you to make something out of that, to get furious and deal with how awful it is that something got in your way. How interesting it would be at the end if you lie down looking at the cigarette and say "Sure" and at the same time be crying. Why should you? Because when you're crying but saying the opposite, it gives you a chance to act! You know, if you're given a chance to act, why do what somebody really expects you to do?

Deal with the nervousness, the peculiarity of the situation, the emptiness, the pain. What makes you say things? Why do you say, "You need this." What do people mean when they say to someone else, "You need this?" They often are thinking about what they themselves need. So it is more interesting for you to be saying "You need this" and playing, "You need this because I need this and nobody gives this to me." Or for you to want her, expect her to say, "You need this, too." But she never says it. Make the work always about the frustrating aspects of what you think you deserve but you do not get. You both got exactly what you asked for in the scene and you can never make a scene — even if the character on stage is the most adjusted, happiest — whatever that may be! — person in the world, unless you want more than what you ask for.

I thought you worked very directly for a feeling between the two of you, what Tennessee Williams would call "the little comfort of love." But there wasn't the dominance of some peculiar things within you that make you wander on that stage, that make you disturbed, that make you upset, that make you excessively happy or excessively unhappy. You were both such normal people up there, which is frightening for any scene and especially for this play! I mean, here's the circumstances: She's goes to bed with the wrong man, he has no way of helping her, the mother has left, she has to do all the work to support them and there is this man following her all around. You really made this an easy task! Rather than finding the peculiarities. It's what Stanislavski says about it taking an effort to sit down. If you really want to sit, you say to yourself "I have to move," and then you sit. If you have to stand you should deal with the fact that "I'm dying to sit down right now." When you're talking it should be, "Oh, if only I would not talk." By doing this, you create an edge within yourself.

Because you have a trained voice, Abigail, you believe in yourself vocally more than you believe in yourself emotionally. You have a tendency of hesitating right before the line. Therefore when the line comes out it doesn't have as much emotional information. The line comes out just fine. The hesitation says "I'm not sure." But then the line is very sure. So if I don't look at that particular moment at the stage, I will never feel that there is any ambivalence. The ambivalence is packaged very nicely, but it is theatrically packaged. Use the hesitation with the words. Once you start with a sentence, you are relentless. Nothing can stop you! Mess up the words more, which I know you can't afford to do when you're singing. But in acting, you've got to mess them up, you've got to let them come out as if the things you're saying are never the things you meant to say. So each word, sentence, moment, has really a lot of subtext, ulterior motives, other meanings.

Imagine things. Imagine that the water you drink is awful, that the house is hot, imagine that the sheets are smelly, imagine that the apartment has an echo, imagine a big nail, your mother put it underneath, so that you can be stepping on nails all the time. You know? Deal sufficiently with the underlying imaginary circumstances — it's kind of interesting, in life some people do it, they believe they're always persecuted. I think you should get persecuted on stage, or you should be wooed when you're on stage. It has to be the sense of exaggeration, the sense of something totally inappropriate one way or another. It's kind of interesting that a lot of the actors we see and that we like are always a little bit more — in a good sense — more neurotic than we would like to be dealing with. Not that directors are not! But with a lot of good actors there is a whole sense of fantasy. Sometimes I'll ask an actor, say, at rehearsal, "How are you?" and he'll say (*Angrily:*) "Well! You didn't ask me yesterday!" That's par for the course. People carry a certain temperament with them and it colors everything they do.

I think you have to allow that paranoia and program the paranoia. With this material it would be wonderful for you to create problems for yourself. Unless they're natural. For everyone that Woody Allen works with it comes naturally. But for a lot of actors it doesn't come naturally. So make your own blocks. If you put a chair in front of the door, there will be something so interesting about opening that goddamn door! Have the things messed up so you can't really reach them. Get something on your hands and have nothing to wipe them with. Find enough problems which will involve you one way or another, and being involved in them will require you to stretch your emotional equipment the way people stretch their vocal equipment by trying to reach certain notes, their physical equipment by working out. You do this by finding a series of physical objects which tie you to the emotional work.

I kept looking at you for what eventually become mannerisms of people. In a good sense. The sort of idiosyncratic things that some actors do when they respond to something happening. I think the more you look at good actors, the more you find out that they come with a bunch of physical and vocal characteristics that someone like a reviewer might call mannerisms, and they become mannerisms when they have no meaning. But if these things are done with a purpose then you identify. And you keep watching, and the people who are functional are just not as interesting. They are just not as interesting on stage as people who develop those other things. And it doesn't come always come naturally, so sometimes we have to help it. The greatest way of helping it is by sending your imagination to a junkyard and collecting the most pathetic, sick details you can ever imagine, you know what I mean? Just bring all that in and let it play on you so that your task somehow becomes to reach for this. Work for physical things. Try to hit things, move things, comb tangled hair. It's interesting what a freezing room does to you, what being covered with a blanket does. If you let the cigarette burn, what does that do to you? Or standing forever and not knowing if she's ever going to talk to you.

Allow all these things to conspire, help stimulate some of the words. Make the *words* active instead of the whole sentence. Try to use the sentence as a series of words. Discover the light as you use the words and text. I think especially you have to watch it because your voices come out so pure that I don't suspect anything. Take time. You really could have made the scene twice as long. It's really kind of — the courage to be foolish up there. You were not foolish. You were precise, you were alive, you were interesting, but you were adjusted people.

So, the strength of the scene was its weakness. Its accessibility helped people watch it, but it didn't help you as actors. It was obligatory acting rather than informed acting. If it was more convoluted, people might not recognize it as easily — if someone would review you they might not "get it" as easily, but it would be more interesting to you because you could discover sides of yourself that you don't know exist. Use the text only as an excuse for you to discover these sides of yourself, as an excuse for the acting work. Don't worry about what it's all about, worry about what *you* are all about.

TO KNOW AND NOT TO KNOW

> *In the climatic scene of Milan Stitt's* The Runner Stumbles, *a nun and a priest find themselves in love and fight against it. The scene brings up one of the most difficult tasks for the actor: how to know and yet not know where the scene is going. Nikos suggests that it is this "knowing" beforehand that minimizes acting, that "tames" and tones down the sort of acting which makes a scene like this alive and interesting.*

NIKOS: It's almost repetitive what we're saying about minimizing certain kinds of acting tasks. This is a scene which starts out about nothing and ends up with feelings. And boy, the two of you were really determined to have this conversation! Unlike what some people said, that they thought you weren't acting with each other, I think you were acting too much with each other. I felt that you were looking at each other, and connecting with each other and flirting with each other so much that I knew exactly what would happen next — because *you* constantly knew what everything you said might possibly accomplish. Like "Oh boy, if I say this or that, it'll really start a relationship between us." All the dialogue in the beginning of the scene was just used as innuendo for the attraction between you, and so I said to myself: "Oh, just stop it and deal with the things you really want to deal with, your love for each other and your attraction for each other and stop wasting so much time talking about the flowers!"

What is essential in material like this is to allow yourselves to be surprised by what happens in the scene. This scene is not about covering something up for us, it is about covering something up from yourself. A scene like this is a very good exercise because there is something there that holds back your immediate acting. Right? The same way in some scenes the actor holds back a certain kind of emotion because that emotion is not supposed to come out in a social situation. Here, because she is a nun and he is a priest, that holds back the expression of their feelings of love for each other. They are holding them down so much that they don't even know that they are doing it. You'll find out the scene makes so much more sense if you really *try* to talk about the subjects, the gardening, the food, and not make them into innuendos for something else.

Now, Sheila, when you came in, you talked to him about the garden as an attempt to please him, so it became social conversation. But if she just comes in and says (*With energy and directness:*) "Here, flowers!" (*Nikos proceeds to act out some of the scene.*) And he says (*Forceful, determined:*) "Yes, that's what I miss, damn it, that's what I miss, flowers!" If you do it that way, then you throw yourself passionately into the conversation about the flowers in order to keep down your passion for each other. Because your task as the character and as the actor is to (*With effort:*) keep — that — down! But you were so goddamn accessible to that passion that it was not interesting when you opened up.

Go completely in the opposite direction. So it becomes (*With increasing momentum and involvement:*) — you deal with this, you deal with that, you keep going, you keep going, YOU KEEP GOING, YOU — KEEP — GOING! And then you feel the need for her and all of a sudden it changes and you say (*Now, whispering, with surprise and emotion:*) "How did I find myself here, how?" And that's why she says, (*Quickly, forcefully:*) "Don't. We NEVER do it again." (*Crying out:*) "We — NEVER!" And then you discover it, you really discover it — (*Openly, loud, with anguish:*) "But why! I feel wonderful with you, talking like that!" It's a wonderful scene for acting because the acting task emerges in spite of yourself, and the emotional thing between them emerges in spite of the fact that you are a priest and she is a nun. Don't be prepared at the beginning of the scene to deal with how you feel about each other. I think if you are constantly prepared to deal with the situation, you are really minimizing your chance for acting. Because then you let it out a little bit at a time (*Hesitantly:*) and a little bit at a time...and a little bit at a time, and all your acting really adds up to nothing. Rather than holding it all back and then letting it all out at once.

It's like an actor picking up the task (*With great effort:*) "I'm not going to cry, I'm not going to cry, I'm not going to cry, no matter how it hurts I am not going to cry." And then the final moment when it all comes out is so kind of fantastic and exciting for you as an actor, *if* you can really make yourself believe that you WILL NOT CRY. Your conversation in the beginning was not about flowers, it was not about eating, it was not about God. It was about a man and a woman who are not allowed to flirt and therefore they are being devious and flirt with the wrong words.

ACTOR: That's the thing I had the most trouble with, finding the line in between allowing myself to love her and hiding —

NIKOS: It is not finding the line in between. It is going all the way out with the opposite. Then the love is a realization that comes *afterwards* rather than during. Because if an acting realization comes during, then it is toned down. So your acting had to be as toned down and your behavior toward each other had to be toned down, because you dealt with truths which you already knew existed between you. And therefore you had to minimize the acting in the scene, because of the nun and priest relationship. Imagine that you do not even *know* that all this potential is in the air between you. All you try to do is deal with a conversation about flowers and eating and God, but for some reason, you find you are dealing with this awkwardly.

ACTOR: The problem I found is that if you allow that to happen too soon, you can't help but notice it.

NIKOS: (*Adamant:*) NO! Not if you are wrapped up in other tasks. Not if you have something positive to be dealing with. And your positive objective is being wrapped up in your own world, you're wrapped up in this task, she's wrapped up in that and all of a sudden you find out that — (*As a discovery:*) "We are talking to each other! And there are a certain kind of feelings…!" You see, when the feelings came, your next line was something like "I want to stop." I said to myself: "Come on, no, you don't really want to stop it, because you've been encouraging it all along!"

With scenes like this, the two characters should proceed on totally different routes. And all of a sudden, you find out that those routes end together and *then* you get upset. And the only way to do that is to make the route you are taking very centered and very exciting. And then you get carried away, you open up to such an extent that when the feeling comes, you find out that there is no escape. But since you knew where the scene was taking you, you were having qualms about opening up. So there was always a little escape for you. And because there was a little escape and because you kept escaping, the confrontation could not be, in acting terms, as exciting.

So. The covers that we *know* are covers are interesting socially but not in terms of an animal behavior on stage. Sheila, you came in already knowing "Boy, is this priest fun to be with!" Rather than saying (*Out there, awkward, letting loose:*) "I don't know what it's like being with him, but when I'm with him, I talk!" And at the end of it you say to yourself: "Does that mean I'm in love with him?" Along the way, as you play the scene, it's as if all of a sudden you find yourself saying things you have never said to anyone. But now you were preparing and adapting it so much that you really knew you were saying all these intimate things to a priest. And you were saying it to a priest who you knew you were interested in and therefore it became in the realm of possibility, and because it was in the realm of possibility the miracle that happens in an acting scene like this was not there. The immediacy was not there.

You kept being puzzled. And in being puzzled you are taming things down. Rather than saying, (*Forcefully:*) "because I'm not confronting this, I'm dealing with that." So you were not active. You did not use the situation as a springboard, you used it as a corset. And because of that you lost some excitement you could have gotten as an actor when, as I say, you keep opening things until you find something. And then you say, "What do I do with it?" rather than knowing beforehand what you are going to find. It's not that you should be trying to surprise us, it's about surprising yourself. When you haven't anticipated it, then you don't know how to deal with it. That's when the acting is alive.

And Sheila, try to take down the little thing in you that is more or less — a constant understanding. I almost felt you have *understanding* if he hits you and *understanding* if he kisses you and *understanding* of this, and *understanding* of that. And that's bad. I just think you should do scenes where you kind of get slapped around. No, you know what I mean? Either get slapped around or get raped, or slap someone else around and rape them. But don't do anything in between, because you seem to be — such a *good job* there. You just seem to be — a happy doormat! And that's really, you know, not very exciting for you. So next time, do something like *The Taming of the Shrew* and make her double. Okay?

COMMENTARY
BY DAVID SCHWEIZER

David Schweizer's first season creating the Second Company at Williamstown led directly to his discovery by Joseph Papp and work at Lincoln Center for Papp's New York Shakespeare Festival. He has continued to direct in New York, at major regional theaters, and internationally with residencies in London, Lisbon, Sarejevo, Stockholm, Oslo, Hamburg, and Warsaw, where his chamber version of Peer Gynt *is still running. He nurtures experimental work with his Modern Artists Company and directs frequently for Mark Taper Forum. In recent seasons he has returned to Williamstown to direct* Present Laughter *and* The Milk Train Doesn't Stop Here Anymore *(with Olympia Dukakis).*

As incredible as it seems, it must be twenty-five years ago that Nikos invited me and some friends up to Williamstown to "get something going" one summer. We were theater-crazed Yalie undergraduates. And one of Nikos' teaching outlets at that point was a Yale undergraduate course in "scene study" or something. It was an acting class, and I was already a DIRECTOR with tons of attitude. But I was privileged to be an invited observer to this galvanized mecca and utterly cool hangout for those of us who were determined to devote our lives body and soul to the theater. Nikos WAS theater to us in 1970s New Haven. He was the theater GOD!

Of course there was the crazy, Martian-sounding Greek accent which he wielded like a machine gun in torrents of opinions and directives. But beyond and beneath that, there was the seductive danger of the man who invented blowing hot and cold — that almost ludicrously atmospheric personal charisma which he served up with gusto for people who were smart or talented or sexy (or, better yet, all-in-one) and shut down cold if he was bored.

It was not a good idea to bore Nikos.

And this is essentially how he taught and what he could impart about the theater. To bore him meant that while you were doing whatever you were doing you were somehow closing off some access to the place where the fresh perceptions and magical impulses reside.

You know what I mean.

You were being less than you could be.

Theater is, God help us, LIVE. And theater artists are always struggling to inhabit the live interactive moment between the performance and the audience. But the best-written scene, the most cleverly staged moment — can go cold. Lifeless. If the communicative urge is not freshly imagined. Nikos' messy, interactive, yet autocratic teaching and directing mode was only about staying awake.

Staying interested. Staying alive.

It was not pleasant to watch Nikos teach or direct on "automatic pilot." In his many years of producing and shaping the summer seasons at WTF there was the inevitable play or event that Nikos had to do just to keep things rolling. They were always a disaster. He had enormous knowledge, startling, almost casual brilliance — but in a sense, not much TECHNIQUE. And technique for its own sake bored him in others.

I was a troublemaker in my youth, a rabble-rouser during my *enfant terrible* years as a youngster director. It was this subversive aspect of Nikos — often well hidden in his later years — that captured my heart and caused me in some measure to capture his. He liked things that caused a little trouble. It kept him interested.

That first summer me and my troupe — shining creatures like Peter Evans, Sigourney Weaver, Alley Mills, and Richard Masur who would later grace so many different stages — made theater in the hallways, hidden recesses, rehearsal rooms in the wee hours of Williamstown. After the initial invite, Nikos gave us virtually no real space or time in which to do anything. Our working hours were spent serving the needs of the grown-up performances on the "Main Stage" — working on crews, carrying "spears." And yet Nikos expected something wonderful and original to happen from us regularly.

Of course it did.

It was his expectation that made it happen.

He knew that.

I decided to do "my own" version of Ibsen's *Peer Gynt*. With five actors. In jeans. No props. Very seventies. Very foolish. The play was one of Nikos' favorites. A sprawling troublemaker of a play. He said nothing. Offered no warnings, nor any encouragement. But he passed by a rehearsal or two in the odd, surprising moment (this was not something he DID, unscheduled — he never had the time) and would look over at me and nod. The glint in his eye brightened.

One memorable midnight we did our "performance" in a rehearsal basement to an exhausted, grumpy company of actors who had staggered dutifully downstairs after some endless performance of their own. (Main Stage shows were inevitably uncut, fully mounted productions of *The Three Sisters* or *Mother Courage* rehearsed in an insane two weeks. See what I mean? STAYING AWAKE, STAYING ALIVE...) At the end of our performance all five actors split up and told a story from the play separately to members of the audience. I looked around for Nikos. I was terrified. *Peer Gynt* WAS ONE OF HIS FAVORITE PLAYS. HE HAD DIRECTED IT. A LOT. I felt suddenly impudent and out-of-my-depth. What could have possibly possessed me? I slipped out of the room as the applause began. Loud. And with lots of cheers!

But where was he?

I found him down the hall around the corner standing quietly. Waiting for me.

The impossibly bright eyes were wet.

He held out his arms. We embraced awkwardly.

"It was, ahhhh…like the beginning of something…ahhhh, something that seems right. Something to give…ahhhh, to the play…"

This was muttered.

He broke away. And swept back into the room to host the little post performance brouhaha and make it somehow his own.

But I, in effect, was made.

Risk. Bravery. And their cost, or reward — the tears of an artist whose soul had been intruded upon.

This was something I could keep forever.

And I would spend my life for better or worse, addicted to the theater.

To staying awake.

Part Four
Breakthroughs

> I long to tremble in front of them with fear, with joy, to speak words full of fire and passion and anger, words that cut like knives, that burn like torches... I want to throw armful of words, throw them bounteously, abundantly, terrifyingly...so that people flare up, shout, rush out... And then I'll stop them. Toss them different words. Words beautiful as flowers. Words full of hope, and joy, and love. And they'll all be weeping, and I'll weep too...wonderful tears. They applaud. Smother me with flowers. Bear me up on their shoulders. For a moment — I hold sway over them all...Life is there, in that one moment, all of life in a single moment.
>
> Tatiana, Enemies
MAXIM GORKY

LETTING GO

> *In this famous scene between Maggie and Brick from* Cat on a Hot Tin Roof, *Nikos deals now with the world of Tennessee Williams as much as he does with specific acting problems. He fleshes out Maggie's and Brick's inner lives and exhorts the actors against accuracy and*

definition in the work. He challenges the actors to let go of purpose and objective, to get "lost" occasionally in order to hook into the enormous need of the characters.

NIKOS: I think in all the Tennessee Williams roles, there has to be a certain inner life, a life that is your secret. For instance, with Brick, we always ask: "Why is this man staying in the room?" Williams is too good a playwright to give you an easy solution. But obviously there is a complicated inner life going on with Brick. I missed that. I thought the work was much simpler and had more strength than I've seen. But I kept wondering what would happen if she never really talked and you existed in that room alone.

There's not one answer, it could be many things for Brick. It could be, "I'm going to stay in the room because I've decided I'm going to torture her because of what she did with Skipper." But as Brick, you have to have a set of emotional circumstances that are as interesting as her world — actually much more interesting because she has so many lines. I mean, in *The Three Sisters,* Solony has only three lines in scenes where everyone else has fifty. So he has to have many more interesting things to play than Tusenbach, because Tusenbach talks a lot.

Alec, I saw you getting annoyed, or upset, or disturbed. But I also saw that if I pulled her out of the room, you would not sit in that room and deal with your liquor, your memories, your plantation. The scene for you got repetitive because you were not dealing with your own life, you were waiting for her to give you something to respond to. You are always in trouble if, when you look at somebody on stage, it is the exact moment the script tells you to look. That means, really, that you have no other world except the unfortunate world of the lines.

The drinking moments, the balancing on one foot, the looking at her with (*Nikos' voice is low and threatening:*) "Don't you dare talk" — these moments cannot just come at exactly the place in the text where the lines indicate that. They can not come in response to exactly what she says and doesn't say. You had a much stronger presence, Alec, but you did not have a world. You really didn't have an emotional scenario that would be so interesting for you that if I took her away, you could live up there, you would exist all on your own. And because of that you became functional many times. Meaning, she serves you, you serve her back, she doesn't serve, you don't serve. When you play the scene like this, you find out that love lines occasionally play as hate lines — whatever that may be! — and hate lines play as love lines. But you were so goddamn accurate. You were very honest, but you were very accurate. You never really said: "I miss you" while you were saying "Shut up." Miranda, you never said, "I want a kid, too!" when you were describing the kids you hate, the no-neck monsters. When you described the kids you were literal with it. But that is not how life works. There is no way for her — when Brick comes in from the bathroom dressed only in a towel — to just describe the kids. Everything you say about the kids, all the details about the biscuit and what they said to Big Daddy — all these things are something about a way of sniffing, a way of connecting. And you try to connect with that and it doesn't work, and you try again with something else (*Nikos speaks faster and more urgently:*) and something else until you finally drop all the ways of beating around the bush and say, "Goddamn it, Brick! Connect!" You find out that accuracy is the worst thing you can do as an actor when you have a scene like this. You know what I mean by accuracy?

ACTRESS: I'm not sure.

NIKOS: You can't afford to be angry only in the angry moments and loving only in the loving moments because then you have no bridge in between. But because all of a sudden the lines are "How about it, Brick?" If your need comes only at the particular moment it appears in the text, then you appear manipulative. No interesting acting happens right on the beat, ever. "How about it, Brick?" should happen in all the moments, for instance, in the moment when you give him the birthday card. So when you ask him to sign the birthday card, it's about that other need too.

Get lost up there. Find moments that you are lost up there. Find moments when what you want to say cannot be emotionally articulated. So that you don't know what to say but you talk anyway and later you think back and say to yourself (*Plaintively, in pain:*) "Shit, I said the wrong thing." So that as the character you don't know how to sit, you don't know how to act. There was such a knowledge on your part — I cannot call it manipulative, because there was something very nice about you both — but it was so programmatic. It was "now we take care of this, and now we take care of that and now we take care of that."

At which particular moment does she use her body? At which particular moment do her fingernails hurt her, at which particular moment does she want to touch the ice he uses, at which particular moment does she want to sit and not deal with it at all? I just think you were so much on the nose when you were asking things. You kept picking up things and shelving them and picking up and shelving them, so that the work did not come out of that constant need which you don't know how to articulate. And therefore some lines will come out like (*Desperately but openly:*) "I'm ugly! I am like a cat! I don't know what to do!" In the course of the scene, in essence, you are trying to find out what is going to work in order to get through to him. I thought you were not finding out, but that you had a plan and were really determined — "First I'm going to do this and then I'm going to do that and then I'm going to do that."

Also, Miranda, you went into a little too much acting — not that it didn't pass, but something tells me you can do more if you do less. There is a little too much out there. I wonder what would happen if you just took that speech and sat there, and said (*Lost, honest:*) "Brick, I'm lonely." I wonder what would happen if you had no objective a few times. As if you'd given up — (*Again, open, lost:*) "Here I am, what can I do?" You try to accomplish things with energy and then the need disappears. And the ambivalence disappears. You know what I mean?

ACTRESS: I think I do. I mean, that would be so liberating in a way because I could, I guess — let go — of all that I think I have to do. That's my problem, really. I can't — (*There is a silence. The actress is on the verge of tears.*) I'm sorry —

NIKOS: (*Triumphantly:*) No, that's exactly it! That's what you need in the scene!

(*The actress laughs a little, and so does the class.*)

NIKOS: Now we see you and you are dealing with something obviously big and important to you: your work. And something hits you and your throat catches. And you can't talk for a minute and you are lost. And that's really it. You know?

ACTRESS (*Soft*): Yes.

NIKOS: I just think there must be a more interesting world in you that is much less definite. I think a year or two from now it might be different — but right now definition is against your best interests. Because you're very articulate about your demands. But the scene deals with frustration and physical need and all these things that can never be said. And what's kind of marvelous, of course, is that all the words she uses come out because of something unspoken about the magic of being together in the room. And at the same time feeling like (*From deep within, whispering:*) "An animal in a caaaaaaaaage!"

I'm not sure that at the end of the scene when she locks the door to make love, that the door can be closed in such a romantic, programmatic way. I'd love just once to see someone playing Maggie go to that door and really slam it! And then see that it doesn't work and then just fall on the floor and say "I'm sorry, it is not really working." You know what I mean, Alec? I'm not sure that Brick's next line (*Nikos says it gently, in a low pleading voice:*) "You're making a fool of yourself" has to be delivered (*Now harsh, abrupt:*) "You're making a fool of yourself." Because if you say it that way it's like you *expect* her to be making a fool of herself.

When these plays were done the first time, they were always cast against type. I just think that your attractiveness, Miranda, was really somewhat professional, because it was placed at just the right moments and it was never out of proportion to what Maggie is asking. I wish you felt very unattractive in some moments and I wish you felt wonderful in some moments, and I wish you felt that he was frustrating you and then at the end of it you say (*Lost, quiet:*) "I don't know what I said. I don't know." And in the process, both of you would have time to really exist in that environment. You know? You existed in the argument, you existed in the debate, but I would love to find out what happens if he was in the bathroom, what you do. The life, the activities, the looking in the mirror, taking off the dress, touching yourself, whatever comes in. The same thing with you, Brick. The drinking, the dealing with the crutch.

Miranda, somehow, somewhere, I wanted you to deal with the fact that you need help. As a person. As a woman up on that stage. That Maggie needs help. I didn't think you needed help. I thought you needed something from him, but I was not inspired to get up and help you at all, you could help yourself just fine any particular moment you wanted, you made that very clear vocally. And in an interesting way, if you go back to all our wonderful actresses, all the good actresses in the American theater are all people who need help! Somebody looks at them and wants to go up there and help them move from stage right to stage left, help them articulate a speech, help them do anything up there! They kind of get lost, they look like lost kids and everybody around them works very hard to help them. So find things that make you lose purpose. I think it's wonderful if you do the whole scene like "I'm a doormat, this is my function." Then you'll see, it will not have the abrasiveness people mentioned.

And Alec, the reason that Brick stays in the room is complicated. Williams himself changed opinions about that many, many times. He's hurting himself by staying in, he's dealing with the father sometimes, he's feeling that he's penalizing her. There's all that. He has as many reasons for staying as Iago has for attacking Othello. And you never know what exactly it is. But there is something, there is a world going on, that is constantly there, that he tries to keep down. Many of these guys in Williams have that, the underneath world that never comes completely out. So reverse it. Promise us much more and give us much less.

ACTING WITHOUT IMPOSITION

The scene is from Sam Shepard's True West. *Even though the work in this scene is more sophisticated, Nikos again focuses on acting problems highlighted by the demands of this particular scene. He talks here about symbolic vs. organic acting and the impositions that actors often create for themselves in order to be "interesting" on stage — as well as those obligations that are imposed by the director.*

NIKOS: If you watch the late-late show on TV and you see some of the old black-and-white movies — before they put color to it! — what's fascinating is that people talk twice as fast in those movies then people do now. The movies now are just (*Nikos pauses for a while and then, languidly:*) "Hello." And twenty-six seconds later somebody has the next line and there is all that pseudo-behavior in between. I assume that if you compare the number of pages of a movie now with an old movie, it would probably be one-third or one-fourth of the number of pages.

But what's interesting in the old movies is that they always find a center through which the speed they use becomes part of acting rather than part of directing. And that was the problem here. I thought that sometimes the two of you were directing yourselves from the results you were getting and I'll explain that. For instance, there was a moment, Jack, where you were taking everything out of your pockets. And the dominant thing was that you were doing this very fast. It was not about what you have collected, or how much each individual thing in your pocket means, or about your great ingenuity in sorting through them — it was just fast. The speed you used communicated something relatively superficial: "I have many things in my pocket." It's the difference — and I don't mean to compare you — but it's the difference between Jerry Lewis comedy and Charlie Chaplin comedy. Chaplin's deals with the fact that the tempo, the speed, or the energy comes out of some function that he has to do. With Jerry Lewis, the tempo, the speed, or the energy comes in because of some kind of imposition, an externally imposed need to do something in a certain way. I felt that both of you had given yourself impositions about the physical attitude and the physical behavior and the way you should carry yourself. So it wasn't your acting that awed us, instead, it was almost like the way you feel at a circus — "Wow, look how fast he did that!"

Many times the decisions you were making on stage were not organically backed up, you were almost forgetting *the reason* certain things were done and therefore your great enjoyment was an enjoyment of *how* you were doing things rather than *what* you were doing. And Jack, I've seen that with you before and I've commented about it. You have such a dexterity in really moving from one face to another, and doing all these performer kind of things, that I think it hurts you. It helps you as a performer but it really hurts you as an actor because it does not allow you to deal with the transitions, the *reasons* you do certain things. I think a lot of the enjoyment we're getting watching you is the enjoyment of surprise rather than an enjoyment that comes out of what we feel. What you did, both of you, is jump from head-step to head-step rather than climb the stairs. So, it was not so much a question of tempo — it was that moments started and ended at the same tempo.

Moments, events, in any scene need to unfold. Then your work becomes human instead of a phenomenon. I was enjoying the more — not necessarily quiet moments, but the moments that —

ACTOR: — were slower.

NIKOS: No, you didn't have to take more time, I don't mean slow down in the scene because the speed of the scene was kind of wonderful. But it was almost as if somebody over-directed you and told you that there is the obligation to do this or that in terms of the tempo. I think it would be wonderful for you not to assume you have to do something anatomically interesting on stage, you know? Because you go into these physical things so fast that you miss for yourself as an actor the reason *why* you move from the one thing to the other. And I think the scene was carried along much more on a kind of imposed necessity to move it really fast, than the necessity of *why* you are moving it so fast. I heard the words as symbols of acting rather than acting. Don't confuse it with the speed because the speed was wonderful. It was just that there was no inner reason for the speed.

I don't want to minimize the fact that the work was very colorful and fun and open and I think that kind of energy is wonderful for actors. But I guess, Matt, I can tell many times what you're about to do and then you do it and it gets fixed. Because there is, as I said, symbolic behavior rather than a behavior growing from something organic. I think you should give yourself a chance to be boring up there. You obviously have a real thing about not being boring, so you kind of keep rushing or you keep hitting things and you loose the trip, you loose the process, you loose the *getting there* from those things.

It's interesting, one of the comments from the class was: "This is easy to watch." That's exactly the problem, the scene was easy to watch. Don't make it easy to watch. Unfortunately people in the theater make things easy to watch because they think the audience is stupid and everyone's so damn tired at night when they go to the theater! But, you know, make it difficult for people. Why don't you make them bend forward to see you and listen to you rather than relax back in their seats? It would be great for either one of you to take the time to say, "I'll just stand here and I don't have to do anything, I'll bore them, but I'll just stand there." You don't have to move from important moment to important moment. Great painters do little things here and there in the painting that they enjoy and nobody else knows what the hell they're doing, and art scholars look at the little corners and say "Look at these little leaves," or you see somebody's name or somebody's moustache. Not everything has to be about the big event, life has a lot in between.

ACTING IN EXCESS

> *Here, watching work he really likes, Nikos speaks about using scale in the service of creating "an organic caricature." He suggests that to create an excessive character and to justify excessive acting, the actor's perception of his problem in the scene needs to be equally great. The scene is from Michael Frayn's* Benefactors.

NIKOS: You know, when we are doing any kind of a play, even if there's a great contrast between the characters, there cannot be a contrast of understanding. The problem, often, when we do a play in this country, is that plays are cast randomly. The director says "I want this person in my cast and I want that person in my cast" without considering how the group dynamic works. That always, as a director, I find very wrong. I try not to do that. I say: "If I can get those ten people together

I'm fine, but if I can't get those four, I'm going to change the other six." It isn't that there is anything wrong with the other six, it's just that the sensibilities of certain actors, the scale of certain actors either match or they do not. You see how this actor goes with that actor, but this other actor doesn't go with the first two at all.

And I think that's the trick of it. I know that sometimes when a production I've done has worked better than I thought it would, or worse than I thought, to a great extent it was because the two people could not play together, you know? But it's more really than choosing actors, it's the way certain people respond to certain people. I thought the two of you were not on the same wavelength. You were on the same wavelength as characters but you were not on the same wavelength as actors. And because of that there was a problem in how the scene balanced. I don't think you were aware, Evan, as much as you should have been in terms of your acting, of the kind of scale that Robert was dealing with in his performance. I wish you had looked at him three or four times and dealt with your response to the kind of over-the-top thing that he was doing, in order to put your work in the same world as his.

Now, Robert, about that over-the-top thing you were doing —

ACTOR: (*Laughing but chagrined:*) I know, I know! I felt like an idiot, I've never done it like that before. I don't know what happened —

NIKOS: No, I thought the work was very good! I found another side of you which I thought was very interesting today. All those physical things, and the scale you had was working very well for you. Before when you've done work like that, I've attacked it because it is decorative, it comes from your sense of musical theater or your sense of the exaggeration of the acting. But I found all that fascinating in this scene, and I would like to encourage you really to go into this organic — and I say this in a very good sense — this organic caricature.

It was very English acting up there. The English take a very bold stroke and use it throughout. While Americans say, "Well, sometimes I'll put this bold stroke in and sometimes I won't" (and therefore we fail when we do that), the English tend to go all the way with it. When you see Derek Jacobi in *Breaking the Code*, I mean, the man goes all the way out. A reviewer might say his work is mannered, and it does turn into mannerisms when the moment does not require it. But for the most part he creates — even though it is a caricature in a sense — an *organic* caricature, and so it works. During the part of this scene when you were standing over him and getting upset, I thought "This is exactly how excesses can become a plus rather than a minus." You really were excessive but because you were so undone and so desperate and so committed to trying to deal with him, all these things were working very well. And all your excesses were really, really on your side and that made for a very alive character.

It's the sort of thing really, not in the same type of a part, that we all love Austin Pendleton for. If anybody else did these kind of mannerisms and other stuff that he does, you'd say "Forget it!" But because he really believes in this, you say, "Oh, that's wonderful!" I just realized — I think it is a matter of the scale of intensity of your acting being equal to the scale of your perception of your problem in the scene. Because your problem in the scene was big, you could get away with murder up there. In a good sense. And when you grew timid and did less, it was not as interesting. But because of the scale of your problem, I was perfectly convinced that the only way to behave in this kind of scene was with all this kinetic excessiveness. This was the first time

I have watched the excessive and, many times, arbitrary things you do, actually work. I have been pushing you more and more toward the simpler things which I think you have been doing, more vulnerability and all that, but this is the first time where I watched your excessive acting make sense.

I think it also has something to do with the content of the material. You know, look at excessive actors. Look at Meryl Streep in *Sophie's Choice* — the problem is so big that it *allows* her to be excessive. And here also — it was something about the hustling of that man, that was very graphically demonstrated, that allowed you to go overboard. And because you allowed it and were determined to really do it and didn't go halfway, it worked.

So I guess what I'm saying is that it's interesting that sometimes we can see the world upside down, and if we're convinced about the world being upside down we can really do whatever we want. I think you seemed very convinced about the physical presence of that man. And because of that, the movement, which was bigger than what I have been encouraging you to do, never appeared decorative, it appeared as part of a necessity for a man who, at the end of it, sweats. He's sweating it because he's doing so much. I'm just saying this because I've seen you many times, and I think it's kind of interesting that you can rewrite your own acting history! And see not only how you can tame some of these things you are doing, which I feel you should do in many scenes, but also in finding roles where this other kind of thing comes out.

I remember when we were working on *Streetcar* with Chris Walken: It was an opportunity for him to use certain acting things that he sometimes does in plays where these things don't belong. I mean he would do some very Stanley Kowalski things when he was in *Ivanov* and you want to say sometimes, "Chris, there are a lot of mannerisms." But then in something like *Streetcar*, because the jackets are leather and the lights are neon, you encourage those very same mannerisms, that kind of kinetic movement. Or in *Pennies From Heaven*, where he can let loose and do all those innate things that are really wonderful.

It's interesting because with dance we certainly believe the excessiveness, you know? I mean, we certainly believe it in people who are quite bold, who tell the story with movement, with dance. I remember seeing Carmen DeLavallade do "Over the Rainbow" with movement, and every time she talked about stars, from what she did with her hands you had a feeling there were two million stars blinking! (*Nikos does a gesture with his hands.*) You know, "STARS!" And you know, it's so fascinating because on a certain level you just say "WHAT!" It's excessive. It's not exactly subtle. But we believe it. It's like some of the people we see on the street, right? We see a lot of people in the street who do some very strange things, and we really believe that more than we do on stage. If we put it on stage, somebody says, (*Incredulously:*) "What is that!?"

But I think the trick of it is finding the scale of the emotional world that becomes once removed from the norm, and then once you're there in that world, then everything goes, then everything is okay. When we did *Uncle Vanya* in Williamstown with Austin, he decided as Vanya to sit on the floor during one of the monologues. And the first time he tried it, it didn't work. But the second time it worked, because he just stayed on the floor forever. He started crawling on the floor, and hitting the floor. And some other actor would not get away with playing on the floor like a kid and hitting and crawling, but Austin's conviction about the emotional necessity of being that kinetic made it fascinating and makes it work.

Now, aside from all this, technically I think you both should do the famous Charles Laughton exercise of throwing a ball at the end of each sentence. Because you do not hit the last part of the sentences, technically. So, by doing that, you are not throwing the cue to the other person. And although sometimes you had a great deal of strength, sometimes you lost it because it is almost as if you slide down rather than aim with the words. You know? And I think it's strictly technical, I don't think it's emotional. I think it's because you run out of energy with the text.

You have to assume that you have not made the point until close to the end of the sentence, right? Because that's what we do, we say to somebody, "Good morning, How are you, are you *fine?*" It's the last part of the sentence that we really use to challenge, or to deal with, or to cope with, in a situation. And that, more or less, is the sort of problem that a lot of the so-called "Method" actors have had. The problem was that they would hit, sometimes, only the center of the sentence, since emotionally the center of the sentence might be more interesting. But by doing that, the challenge in the text has not always been there. Aim it. Aim with the words and don't look away until you're sure they've hit.

MESSING IT UP

> *Chekhov scenes are best realized, Nikos suggests, by the actor focusing on the "life" of the scene, rather than the words the characters say to each other. His description of the "life" in this particular scene from* Uncle Vanya *(between Sonya and Yelena) is chaotic, unpremeditated, and messy. "Mess it up" was one of his favorite exhortations in the classroom — and especially with Chekhov.*

NIKOS: I thought both of you made yourselves very available, and I thought, [*Yelena*], it was a great improvement from the last time. Unfortunately, though, it became a scene about lines rather than life. What Robert said was very right about something needing to be messed up in the scene.

To take a very obvious example: When you come in, Sonya says: "The doctor was here." And you say: "Let's drink wine, let's drink to our friendship." This moment could have many things: Two people running toward the wine, one person trying to find a glass, the glass is dirty, the other person picks up the other glass, you try to pour, she takes it back, somebody's spilling the wine, somebody's wiping the other person with a napkin, etcetera, etcetera. The reason I'm saying that is not because I'm trying to add business, but it can't be a scene about people talking. There is nothing as dull as two people talking! Really! Unfortunately, it's considered a very interesting thing in the world right now for everyone to just, you know, talk. But this is not a very interesting thing to put up onstage.

For instance, take Sonya's first speech. You really didn't have to look at yourself in the mirror to deal with the line "How awful it is that I'm not beautiful." If the playwright gives you a speech all by yourself, why would you deliver the speech in the same way you would've delivered it if there was someone else in the room? Right? I mean, here is your chance! (*Nikos lets loose, acting it out:*) "There's nobody watching me, I can just stuff myself with grapes, I can get fatter and fatter and fatter because he doesn't like me anyway, I can bang on the piano, I can run around." You know? "And then I come out of church and this awful woman says I look bad! I look bad! (*Long, drawn out:*) I — don't!" If you're going to do something with the mirror, smash it or put the mirror down so that you don't have to look yourself in the mirror. But looking at yourself in the mirror and then saying that you're not attractive is — stupid. You know what I mean?

When doing a monologue, you should know what happened immediately before. This is going to be the springboard of the speech, but it is not the full context. I call this 'time-given circumstances,' which has its own depth before the speech. There is a tricky way of doing it for interpretation or for doing it through your soul. Good actors don't use time-given circumstances for the interpretation, they always use them to really get going. That's why it's so wonderful to work with someone like Blythe Danner, who, no matter what the situation, turns time-given circumstances into an advantage for her acting. Everything is a springboard for her to be fuller as an actress. You could say, "Oh, let's not see the scene this way, let's see it that way," but she would still use either direction as a springboard, though a different kind of springboard each time. If you can use the circumstances as a springboard rather than a corset, you're okay. They will not limit you, they will give you freedom.

Now, Yelena, you come in, and Sonya looks at you. And you don't know what to say, you walk all around the room, and you think, Well, what do I say to her? Okay: "The storm is over, you know." And she doesn't say anything. And then you say, "Why are we enemies, I want us to be friends." And so, what should you do with that line, "I want us to be friends?" I mean, you did absolutely nothing except you stood there and said "I want to be friends!" A lot of people can stop you on 42nd Street and say "I want to be friends," but you certainly are not going to follow them, dear! Are you? So there must be something else that you do. I mean, is it an embrace? Is it kneeling, is it sitting on the couch and calling her to you, is it wrapping a scarf around her? There are many things and it doesn't really matter what you pick. But the reason you need those physical things, at least for a while, is that they will make the scene much more informal for you.

I mean, you had that drink in your hand but you never drank it! How much more interesting if every time you were embarrassed you would drink a little bit more because you're upset because she's talking about Astrov. And, [*Sonya*], you kept looking out the window! If I were her, I would grab your face and say "Sweetheart, Sonya, stop looking out the window, it makes you appear crazy!" You kept looking out the window — why, I don't know!

There are so many things! Why didn't you think about adjusting yourself on the sofa, why didn't you think of cuddling up, why didn't you think of just throwing your apron over your face while you talked, because you're blushing, why didn't you think of getting behind Yelena and thinking: "You look so lovely I just wish I was as lovely as you are!" Why didn't you think of trying to start picking things up on a tray and running out with them? Now, what these things would do to you — they would not be gestures — they would give you constant activities.

You could tickle each other, you could fix each other's hair, you can throw scarves around each other, you can pour more wine. You run to pour the wine because it's about to become exciting when [*Sonya*] says "Tell me something about him, would you please?"

Now, it is not for you as an actress to think that I want that line faster or slower, or with more this, or more that. To think about it that way makes it artificial. Instead, think of something that you want to *do* for her because she's going to tell you all the things about Astrov that you want to know. It'll make it more interesting for you if you run over here — run, pick up the bottle, and say, "Tell me something about him."

Our problem always, is that we assume that we do not have demons to control, we really assume that we are there to talk and that we don't have to *earn* the right anew for somebody to be listening to us. And you earn that right only when you are creating situations on stage that deal with an overall life. Even sitting on the sofa is not that interesting, I wish one of you was on the floor and the other on the sofa, I wish both of you would cuddle together, I wish both of you would start hitting each other. At the very end, Sonya, when you came back in to tell her she could not play the piano, you telegraphed it from the moment you came in, and then walked very slowly over to her. By the time you reached the piano, I said "Oh, come on, please tell her, get it over with!" because I already knew a long time ago what you were going to say. Run to her, and then say the line! Or the two of you could've embraced each other, you could've started screaming, you could've shut the piano on your fingers.

Now, the reason we need those things is not to demonstrate visually what goes on emotionally, but because it is a scene about relationships, it's a scene about embraces, it's a scene about tears, it's a scene about handkerchiefs, where the words come in accidentally. So I'm not really saying, guys, in case of doubt, add props. What I'm really saying is that in case of doubt, find situations that make the conversations incidental and the life imperative. Well, look, it's really like the simple matter of singing in the shower, you know, I am told that people feel better singing in the shower. I don't really *know*, because I wouldn't do it! But people feel this, so they sing, and then the singing really becomes something else, because it's together with the water and the soap and whatever else, and it comes out in an accidental way.

It was very, very difficult, really, for the two of you, to make the scene exciting. You made the scene comfortable for yourselves, and I thought both of you were very appealing, as everybody said, and very attractive and honest with it. But you would not abdicate the rules, you would not give permission to yourself to get involved in a kind of situation where the lines would be incidental to the life.

So it was became a discussion, rather than sharing secrets, complaining, crying, laughing, opening your souls. I don't know what your operative words were for the scene, but never make a scene about talking, make it always about something else. It would be wonderful if you made it a scene about two women getting drunk. You know what I mean? Because all the secrets would come out. Why do you think there are so many movies where two women go to the ladies room and put lipstick on together in front of the mirror? I mean, how many movies do you see with that? I just saw the play *The Women* in London, and that's all it was, they kept disappearing and gossiping, with a great sense of fun. Find, create for yourself the conditions where the lines are inevitable and possessed. They are inevitable, they come out because silence is wrong for the situation, and possessed because they have a kind of a point of view that comes not from the text but from the situation.

The same thing when you went to play the piano, Yelena. You certainly could've looked through the music, suppose the stool was too low, or you had to open the seat to find the old music that you didn't remember, suppose you had to take off all your rings, your wedding rings to play the piano and it became like taking off all your shackles, and your shawl comes off, as if you want to make yourself naked. Suppose the goddamn piano was dusty and you just kept dusting it and you thought you were taking all the dust from your soul! Because then you would create the conditions.

And you'll find out it happens all the time; in life it happens much, much more. I mean, I found out when I was doing *The Glass Menagerie*, I remember the first few days when I started giving notes to Joanne Woodward — who is so brilliant — and she would go to the bouquet of flowers on the set and she would start cutting all the dead leaves, and after the fourth or fifth day I realized what it was. I said, "Wait, don't get nervous now, don't play with the flowers, let me give you the notes." It was a kind of a thing she did that said: "Well, I'm listening to the notes but it is not going to hurt me hearing the notes, because I can do this thing with the flowers." Everyone is constantly doing things in life that are connected to a whole psychological world, up to the time that you stop them and say, "Hey, wait, why are you doing that? Analyze yourself and tell me why you're doing this or that." But you must give yourself permission to do these things. In movies, where because the situations are often so drastic, you find out how much dialogue changes from the page to the screen. Because it is delivered in overblown situations. Add those things. Find the freedom to do those things.

When you say "Let's become friends," let that play. That's a biggie. Let it play not as text, but in touching each other, embracing, dancing, sitting on the floor, throwing a couple of pillows at each other. I don't know, it can change every day, so don't think of these things as interpretive. And then the lines will come out fully. You see, what you don't want the audience to be able to do at the end of the scene is remember lines. Only in Shakespeare do you want that. The rest of the time, the more lines they forget from the text the better off you are. I mean the best thing would have been if the class had said "Oh, the scene was about two women hugging each other." I mean even if a couple of people say it's a scene about two lesbians, that would be great, because that would mean you've done something that established another world. Or it can be that this is a scene about drinking, or two very silly, giggly people. But it should never be: "This is a scene about a woman who said this, and another woman who said that." You've got to forget the text in order to live it.

COMMENTARY
BY BONNIE MONTE

As Artistic Director of the New Jersey Shakespeare Festival since 1990, Bonnie Monte has directed such plays as The Homecoming, Electra, The Sea Gull, Twelfth Night *and* A Midsummer

Night's Dream. *During the 1980s, she was Associate Artistic Director of the Williamstown Theatre Festival, assisting Nikos in the entire artistic and organizational sphere of WTF. She also helped produce several joint ventures with other major companies:* Sweet Bird of Youth *at the Royal Alexandra Theatre in Toronto,* A Streetcar Named Desire *at Circle-in-the-Square and* The Glass Menagerie *at The Long Wharf Theatre. She is a member of the faculty of Drew University and was honored with New Jersey's Women of Achievement Award.*

For eight years, I spent most of the days of my life with Nikos Psacharopoulos. It was a great privilege and adventure. As I look back on it now, it takes on somewhat mythic proportions, as though the Gods of the theater decided one day to bestow a great gift on me by carving my path to intersect with his. Knowing Nikos so intimately was a fate reserved for few, and one, I say with some pride, that only the thick-skinned and hardy could endure. He was *not* user-friendly.

There is no question that my time with Nikos was the defining "moment" in my life as an artist; it was also the most difficult of trials, and the most rewarding of friendships and collaborations. This duality of experience or characterization is often employed by many in an attempt to define Nikos — to articulate who he was and how he operated. Jean Hackett's apt and eloquent description of him in the introduction to this book is filled with contradictions because that is really the only way to come close to the essence of Nikos. You could never predict anything about him and that certainly kept you on your toes. You could only be sure that the minute you were complaining about him, he would suddenly appear behind you, out of nowhere.

The lessons and "breakthroughs" I took away with me from my years at Williamstown are worth their weight in gold, and I have strived every day of my life to live up to the level of passion and adventure that Nikos nurtured in me and in all those lucky enough to work with him. My history, then, is peppered with breakthroughs, artistically and personally. I came of age under his tutelage, and there is no question that it was indeed often a case of "drop by drop, knowledge comes to the unwilling."

Not a day has gone by since Nikos left us that I have not thought of him, but it has been quite some time since I have closely reexamined my day-to-day existence with him. In struggling to write about him now, I find myself frustrated at the difficulty of relaying the profundity of his teachings. My "study" then was different than most. I am not an actor, I am a director and an artistic director. My process of learning, however, was essentially the same as that of the actor's process with Nikos. One had to rise to the occasion, one had to be courageous, one had to be willing to fail, one had to invest body and soul. These was no room for even momentary lapses of commitment. One had to seek and strive and fight for breakthroughs, otherwise you risked boring him, disappointing him, and angering him — and by extension, yourself. The investment was everything, and if you made it there was great reward.

Of the hundreds of quotes that emanated from and were circulated about Nikos, there is one that sums up, for me, the core of Nikos' vision and persona. It is a line from Tennessee Williams' masterpiece *Camino Real,* one of Nikos' favorite plays. A play, incidentally, in no small way about breakthroughs. It goes like this: "Make voyages! Attempt them! There's nothing else!"

The willingness to lead those voyages made him larger than most, even though he was not a big man. He was often, as I heard the actor Tom Brennan describe him, "a force of nature." I try to live by and instill in others Nikos' unrelenting admonitions to be brave, to commit, to risk, and to explore. *Everything else*, I have learned, is a voyage not worth taking.

In *A Streetcar Named Desire,* Blanche Dubois says, "And then the searchlight which had been turned on the world was turned off again…" When Nikos quit this earth, for a very long time I felt abandoned in darkness, but "drop by drop" grief turned into the desire to voyage again. And then, in what was for me a seminal breakthrough in my life, the light of Nikos' legacy burst forth again, and I have never felt it wane since.

PART FIVE
Artistic License

> Everything she does is her own. She has had only one school: life; she has formed herself through the observation of life, through the understanding of life. The simplicity of this Italian woman is the fruit of extreme complexity. It is simplicity achieved through the penetration of the whole…
>
> Russian critic Suvorin
writing on Eleonora Duse

PROMISE

In this scene from the film Julia, *Nikos talks about the inner life of the actor, the promise of the emotional range the actor holds within which is never completely revealed. He suggests that this inner promise is fundamental to great acting, and must always be stronger than the acting in the scene.*

NIKOS: As artists, what you have to do is to conjure the *promise* of what is there, right? It is like a dollar bill, a dollar bill is absolutely nothing. But the piece of gold that it represents which used to be in

Fort Knox is much more interesting, because that's the thing that has value. The dollar is just paper. In the same way, it is not interesting when the acting is stronger than the life it represents, but when it is a kind of promise, a frustration within you about the myriad of things you want to do out of which you get to do only one. It is that kind of promise that makes for great acting, the idea that all good actors are unfinished actors in terms of coming backstage and saying "Goddamn it, I didn't do it well tonight." That is absolutely accurate, because good actors always have something more to do, and something more to do than they ever really do on stage. The moment they accomplish their task, they stop being good actors. That it why I am always saying that good acting is not about accomplishment, it is about a promise.

Don't get tempted by the idea of: "This is heavy, and we're going to have to talk about it, it's difficult." That's bad because once you have prepared yourselves and us that what you're about to say is difficult, then when you say it, it's not difficult anymore. Once you have done that preparation for the line physically, it removes all the energy and all of the need. You have demonstrated something and, I suppose, in a way you feel better for it. That's, I guess the basis for — whatever they call it — scream therapy. You scream "Ahhhhhhhhhhhhhh," and you say "Thank God I screamed, I feel so much better." But, really, if you have inside you that scream and you never use it, that's when it — acting — gets interesting.

If you're sitting down when you always want to stand up, or if you stand up when you're dying to sit down, that's what interesting acting is. Interesting acting is not when you do everything you want to do, because then you do things mechanically. If you are avoiding looking at each other it is not interesting, but if you are looking at each other, wanting to talk and being unable to, wanting to move and being unable to, then you can create an edge within yourself.

This is a wonderful acting scene for two women. And what's fascinating, first of all, in a more superficial way, is the situation itself. They are at a restaurant trying to keep their conversation a secret from the Germans who are watching them, right? If the Germans see these woman doing a lot of acting, they'd grab them, it would be curtains for them! But because both Fonda and Redgrave are such brilliant actresses, they did not only deal with the fact that the Germans would get them, but the idea that, emotionally, they had so many more things to say and so much more love to part with than they could ever get to use in the situation.

To take an obvious example, Vanessa Redgrave's character has a line where she tells Jane Fonda's character that she has a wooden leg. And she says it with a smile. And that smile makes the reality of her having a wooden leg so much more frightening. If you say (*Pityingly:*) "I have a wooden leg," then the other person and those of us out in the audience are tempted to say "Good!" But the most interesting thing is the fact that the tragedy, the implied human tragedy in any situation, is related to courage.

You had a great sense of who these two women are. You both took your time and were more emotionally available then I've seen you before. But, still, it was in some way more about the accomplishment of the task, rather than the effort. It is the effort to smile, the effort to appear in a certain way, the effort to deal with an urgent world that nonetheless is not as important as the world within you. When there is a promise underneath, it becomes a question of saying that you know words are so silly, and even acting is silly when the thing that you have underneath is so important. And when what you have underneath is so much bigger than the fact that you are acting, you forget you are acting and the audience does too.

PHYSICAL COMEDY

In critiquing this scene between Amanda and Elyot from Noël Coward's Private Lives, *Nikos suggests that comedy exists not just in words, but in the body. It is the physical life of the scene that frees the actor to respond to the material in a visceral, rather than a mental way. Nikos goes on to catalogue various physical techniques used by different comic actors in different plays.*

NIKOS: Comedy, all good comedy has always been very based in the physical, that's why comedy works so well in silent movies. We forget that even when a comedy exists on the verbal level, that parallel physical world is what takes us along, what makes us abandon logic and go along for the ride. I think about *Room Service* that we did at Williamstown with the funniest actors ever: Joe Grifasi and Dick Cavett and Jimmy Naughton and Ed Herrmann. But when I remember it, I don't remember funny lines, although I know the lines were funny. What I remember is those guys coming in and out of all those doors, and Joe Grifasi carrying a moose head in and out of those doors.

You made the material sound very funny — you really did. But you need to make it *feel* funny, too. Both of you were very intelligent up there, and it was great for us to see two intelligent people rather than two dummies! And it was wonderful because you took something that was sufficiently exaggerated and made it very honest, rather than taking honest things and making them exaggerated which has been your pattern. I just wondered why you did not go further with the physical tasks. I think the basis of any kind of exaggerated play is to do the impossible but in a very possible manner.

It needed more physical things from both of you in terms of who you are as characters, so that it would not just be a free-for-all vocally, but also a free-for-all physically. I wish there were more pronounced arguments, and I wish there was more pronounced wooing — in terms of the physical behavior.

I don't want only to listen to you. I want to watch you. It's really the difference between talking it and living it. The way in a good production of Noël Coward there is always a pillow fight. And in a good comedy, there are always some physical things supporting and going parallel to what you feel, so it is not so much all about language. Now of course, if the comedy is by George Bernard Shaw one can afford to go totally verbal because it is so overwritten in terms of the situation and because his thought process is so dazzling. But in a lot of these English comedies, you want to go for the physical freedom, as if the comedy exists in your bodies as well as in your words. You see, these characters are people who *perform* their feelings. The performance of the feelings depends not just on the verbal dynamics but the physical dynamics, the repetition of certain things.

I thought you did the argument extremely well. You were both very alive and very interesting. You made yourselves very attractive as people which is very important. I think in material like this, unless the people are attractive — and I don't mean in terms of looks, although you both are — but in terms of doing the specific behavior with a kind of confidence, and doing it in a way that makes people want to look at you. But I think that you used only the verbal ammunition, rather than saying, "What country do they come from, how do they physically do these things?" Without making it inorganic.

You see, it almost takes old-fashioned acting. You know? In terms of the physical moves. I'm just reading the new biography about the Lunts, and it's so fascinating, from looking at the photographs in the book to think about the things they must have done. A bird would go by and they both would see it, or first one would see it and then the other, in the middle of a scene that had nothing to do about a bird. They just put it in. And you say to yourself, they did all that junk, all those really dreadful plays, but you understand why everybody wanted to go and watch them. Because it was not just verbal theater, it was physical theater, it was about entrances and exits, it was about two people sitting in tandem and standing in tandem; about somebody chasing somebody else, about a whole other world. And I feel that's something you could examine. Then I think you both would do very well, because you would not depend always on your verbal 'game-ness,' and you would not depend always that it's all up here, in your head. Too much of it happens up here, because you are not letting other things happen with your body.

I think it would be wonderful for you both to do something that's really crazy physically. And take it for granted that you can do it. A dancer jumps way high with a smile, it just doesn't hurt her, and she doesn't doubt it when she jumps. It appears done beautifully — sometimes even when it is not! In comedy, the physical and the vocal are like parallel theatrical games. It's just using other means — having so many things available to you, many impossible things you can do possibly, rather than having to totally depend on yourselves. Set up situations, with a myriad of physical things around to help you. The way in a realistic, serious play, we rely on an environment. So that you don't have to come up with all the acting yourself, you can touch something, you can smell something, you can wander and drape on furniture, you can drink, you can open the window, you can smoke, you can serve tea and coffee and pour and spill and if you're in an Ibsen play you dust furniture and arrange dried flowers! And it gives you more than just talk to base your acting on.

WORDS AND DEEDS

> *Hampton's* Les Liaisons Dangereuses *begins with a scene between Merteuil and Valmont. Merteuil tries to convince her former lover to seduce a teenage girl in order to get revenge on someone else, and offers herself as a reward if he succeeds. Valmont declines her offer and reveals that he is much more interested in another woman, the virtuous Tourvel. In this critique, Nikos discusses the specificity of both the scene and the play in terms of the kind of inner life the actor needs to meet the demands of the circumstances and the language of the play. With most material but especially here, the actor's challenge continues to be uncovering the life that the text represents.*

NIKOS: I saw this play first in London in a very small space. What was interesting about Alan Rickman was the fact that he was cast so accurately. It was just like, in essence, he didn't even know if something he said was either morally bad or good. It was the *activities* that were bad or good. And obviously even though there is a great struggle between the two characters, there is also a struggle within themselves, too. How much do you want to become vulnerable and how much do you not want to become vulnerable? How much are you excited about having her and how much is she excited about having you, or how much are you disgusted? It can be any of these, but whatever it is, it's not really about words. I've seen the play twice, and after seeing it the first time I never remembered the words. The second time I went back, I went back to hear it, I wanted to hear the text. But then you realize the play's strength is the situations and not the words. Also in London it was in a very small theater, the stage was lower and the set almost worked in that production because it didn't look like a Macy's window, the way it did here! When you walked out from the play and you just said "Wow, what a world we live in!" Rather than "Wow, what kind of language we hear!"

I kept trying to think why I was not as interested in the scene as I should have been. Both of you were relatively at ease up there, and I think the intelligence came through and the essence of the overall play came through. But I was missing was the specificity of the situations. Now, sure, these characters are playing a game, but why are they playing the game? I think the playwright reminds you many, many times that there is something in that 'game-ness' that is perverted, sort of wildly — abnormal! And this perversion is not in the dialogue but in the *actions* that the characters have done, or are doing, or want to do. The scene we saw now was the dialogue of naughty people, but your actions were not those of fundamentally dirty people. You were very clean-cut up there, guys, you know?

Mertueil says to him, "I have a job for you. I want you to make love to this young girl. She's fifteen and she's a virgin and this and that. Now, will you get her?" And then Valmont comes back and says, "No, but I'll tell you why. Because I want someone else, someone else who's much younger than you are, someone who is virtuous, which you are not, someone who is pure, which you are not, and that is the one I'm going to get." It's not about the naughty expression of what he wants, the naughtiness in having sex with someone, but about the prohibitive action of saying to her: "I want something, and it's not you."

And then she says, "If you degrade yourself a little more, if you agree to sleep with this very young girl, there is a reward that I will give you." Now she obviously means the reward is that she will let him have her sexually. But in the moment in this scene when you are dealing with that sexual reward, we should have a feeling that something might happen right then, you know? You were very naughty and playful with the language but the actions that I imagine behind the words were not really very naughty. There was not that danger behind it. Valmont says to her: "Look, with you it is cold, it is indifferent, I miss passion when I'm with you." But I didn't feel it was dangerous for you to hear that. I didn't feel you thinking, "Oh, wow, I'll get you for saying that." The verbal pyrotechnics worked for you in the scene, and I thought it was interesting for you, Vicki, to have the upper hand, since you usually seem to like to play victims! But somehow in the air, in the 'gameness', in the playing with each other, there was not that thing about two animals who would just kind of touch some live thing and then kill, devour.

In my memory now of your work I associate the scene with words, I do not associate the scene with activities. I did not associate with him seducing a fifteen-year-old girl, I did not associate with her cruelty to the other man, I did not associate it with any kind of destructiveness on the part of these two. The scene got very lyrical and very romantic. There was a great deal of romance to the scene and there was never a sense of how perverted their feelings are. I hate to say that because you weren't really playing it that badly, but because it lost its specificity the scene really became a little bit like college kids talking about sex. You know? Rather than two people determined to destroy each other because of the inner problems. And the inner problems are obviously something about the love and the lust that you have for each other and what really happens when love turns a corner and becomes something that destroys itself and destroys the other person.

You know, this is not a play about *a lack* of morals. Because that would not be interesting or dangerous enough. It's about *perverse* morals. It's not about people who are amoral, it's about people who are immoral. Not in terms of words, but in terms of deeds, because they think in a certain kind of way. And in an interesting way it isn't even about that. The center of this play is really about — the closest thing is *Richard III* — (*Nikos paraphrases.*) "I, who cannot become a lover, I will now destroy. I have laid plots, I have manipulated, I have done all of these things in order to destroy." I mean, you were both very charming but you were not vulnerable to the problems of this particular — sick! — love and therefore the specificity of the scene was lost.

I'm not sure it's important who's winning. What's important is *why* do you want to win and how, when you're winning, you're really also losing and what are you losing when you're winning? And finally you say, "I want one thing if I succeed — you!" And the other person thinks, "Oh, wow, it's going back to that!" That's the danger territory. So it's just like animals, sniffing all around, stalking, watching, and moving in for the kill. And there is an enjoyment, a 'game-ness' to that. I felt the scene got general because in this play the specific moments about the passion, or the love, or the tension require you to look at the world upside down. And what's interesting about these characters is not that they *talk* about the world upside down but that they *look* at the world upside down.

I just felt like you distanced yourself from, number one, the implicit actions; and, number two, the reasons that those actions are interesting for you. By becoming charming it became general. And the charm is there, but obviously the thing underneath is very frightening. It is not about people who talk cynically, it is about people who talk just fine. But when you imagine their acts, those are the acts of cynicism, you know what I mean? It's about having a great, creative passion about destructive things. It's almost like somebody saying "I press a button and kill that many people." It's about somebody slapping somebody who cannot move, and somebody kicking someone and somebody stepping on someone. There is a crispness, a deadliness, about the activities. And I thought you were so carried away with the charm and the fun and the 'game-ness' — that at the end of it I had a feeling about what great folks you are to have at a party, but I could not really imagine you in the situations.

I guess what I'm saying what I've said many times — the reason things become interesting is that the life represented is always more interesting than the text. And that the really good actors have an ability of communicating that to you. Sometimes they don't even think about that, right? Many, many times we know very good actors who haven't thought of this or that, but they communicate that sense to it. And that's when it gets interesting, when the life communicated is more interesting than the form, or the text that you're using. Then it has more anxiety to it. And I just felt that the life was cheated, because the scene was fun and colorful and elegant, but something about your personal life, the fact that this is a matter of life or death, the fact that if one person moves closer something dangerous will happen — was missing. It's a play where the two of you going to bed together would be — like a knife. It would be either the agony or the ecstasy but nothing in between.

I mean, really, there must be a lot of animosity in that woman. He says to her, "You're only seeing one man, that's boring." But she's never going to show that this is boring her because she's not going to give him that satisfaction. It is very boring for her probably; after the scene is over she just goes upstairs and cries, but she's not going to let him see that. She says "What do you suggest for your reward?" And he says: "You!" And it's like: "You son of a bitch, you're not going to try to control me again, I'm not going to get mixed up with you because that's dangerous. Screwing with a fifteen-year-old kid is not a problem, but with you it's going to become dangerous, and I would rather have my independence than my joy."

It's much, much more convoluted than either of you ever suggested with your acting. The needs and the vulnerabilities and the anxieties and the joys and the potential danger makes the suspense — it's really is a great duel with people throwing knives and not knowing who's going to be hurt next and getting occasionally hurt. I mean, getting cut up and bleeding on the stage. And until you get that, it becomes about manners, not needs. In London they eliminated all the different sets and did the play with just one set which was wonderful, because it was written as a collage. And I'd think you'd find that even this scene is a collage.

So, the images of what you are doing have to be clear and specific, progress and retrogress throughout with an unbelievable amount of personal involvement. There is a constant choice of being nasty, or being loving, and when people move back and forth between these it usually happens because of some kind of major problem! You know, granted, it is a French novel, but because it's been adapted by an English person the play doesn't come across as nonchalant. It's not that very French thing that's like "out of nothing better to do, we do this." It's a choice about certain strains of — diseased — sexuality that gives it the specific passion.

POINT OF VIEW

The play is A Streetcar Named Desire; *the scene is the morning after the poker game that ended in a drunken brawl with Stanley hitting Stella. Blanche has spent the night upstairs at a neighbor's. Stella, however, returned to Stanley in the middle of the night. In this scene, Blanche confronts her sister about her relationship with her husband. In his critique Nikos deals both with textual elements and the acting task of developing a set of inner monologues that spell the relationship between the sisters. He talks about the need for prejudicial acting, the point of view of the actor in the circumstances of the scene.*

NIKOS: Wonderful. Really very good work. Nadia, the moments that you weren't censoring, like the kneeling moment and the waking up moment and the moment that you were telling her what your needs were, I thought were spine-chilling. In terms of the vulnerability it was the best I've seen you do. And Katherine I thought the freedom was very good, you were much less self-protective in this than you usually are.

But I kept thinking that many times you both were shelving your needs, and because of that you were stopping the life of the material. I wish both your inner monologues were stronger. You kept waiting for the other person to feed you completely, and you fed from the other person so well that your own inner life just kept disappearing.

It's interesting, Nadia, that at the beginning you just kind of sat down and the air was let out. You completely dropped what you came in with, rather than having an continuous inner monologue of "But why, Stella? But why, but why?" I mean this scene — really any kind of scene — is two interrupted monologues. And you should assume that you have a monologue and she does too and accidentally, the other person might come through with a line during yours. There's a continuity. But now, Blanche would throw you something, Stella, and she would floor you. Completely, as if you had no idea who Blanche was! It was as if your subtext was all about being amazed, shocked, that Blanche would say the things she said. Rather than playing a subtext of, "I know Blanche, Blanche is going to say things like that, and I'm fighting to keep Blanche from interfering with me and Stanley," or "I love Blanche and I hate to upset her, but I'm trying to get her to stop interfering with my life."

The scene was without a history, you know? You had to build it up moment by moment, instead of than having the basis of all the prior moments that have happened in your life, and coming in prepared. I think scenes are much more interesting if you come in prepared for something and you don't get it, rather than if you come in and realize something isn't there.

For example, Nadia, though I found that first moment fascinating, I think it took away from your need to reach her. And by the time you realized that Stanley wasn't there, there wasn't enough energy left for your conversation with her. But if you had just been *waiting* up there — I don't remember how they did it in the movie, but I just think it's great if Blanche has been pacing up and down and up and down waiting and waiting for Stanley to go, she's just been up there for three or four hours and then, having seen him go, she runs in and yells (*Nikos lets loose:*) "HAS HE GONE???" (*The class laughs.*) Because then it is almost like "I have been postponing my need forever!"

It's sort of the order in which you pick up the many threads of the scene. It's always interesting if in a scene you pick up not the thread of the first line on the first line, but the thread of the tenth or fifteenth line on the first line. Because you didn't do that, therefore you kept finishing your tasks. And as I have said many, many times, great acting comes from what is unfinished, not what is finished. Because if it is finished there is no need to make an effort. In effect, you kept analyzing the scene rather than synthesizing the scene. This makes for fascinating acting, but your motor could not go all the way. It's like saying "Look, I don't want to talk now," but the conversation still goes on. That conflict in you builds the emotional need.

You both got surprised by the fact that the other actor dealt with a certain element of life rather than assuming that's what the other person would do. That's what I mean about coming into the scene with a history. And I think, Katherine, two or three times you let out the air. You sighed, and then the line came out, and that sigh cut down your inner motor, which should be: "Please don't talk about it, please don't talk about it, I'm happy, I don't want to lose my happiness," or whatever you choose. Consequently lines were tested against an open void, everything was a discovery — which in a way gave your answers an immediacy, but you were not giving prejudicial answers, the way we really do in life.

It's amazing the way we really are in life — if someone starts doing something you respond immediately, you get upset, or you get elated or whatever. That is because you have a blueprint of life within you which the other person doesn't know. So if they connect with the magic word something happens and if they don't connect with the magic word, it doesn't. I felt you were missing those magic words, so when Blanche says "Stanley" you jump at it, inside. You go (*Sharply:*) "What about Stanley?" Or when Stella says "beer" or even touches a beer bottle, Blanche has a reaction.

Nadia, it would have been wonderful if the information had piled up more for you, because when that happened at the end it was very touching. Very naked work. But it would not have hurt if it were more repetitive. You have an agility which I think hurts you as an actress, because in your repertoire you have too many things. You try that, and then you take something else, as if you have just one scene to get them all in. You will find out that stage time doesn't move as fast as you move. You move faster than stage time, you are like a Concorde up there! You know what I mean? It's just amazing how quickly you get something and how quickly you adjust and occasionally you're two steps ahead of your own emotional world. You should allow yourself to brood more. You know what I mean by brood? I think there has to be a creative brooding up there.

Katherine, what you played was "Do I have to cope with her?" You were making it clear that the tasks you had were stronger than what you wanted to deal with. But as an actress it's more like — you welcome more obstacles and you welcome more fights and you welcome more conflicts. You know, Cyrano's great line: "Give me giants! I will kill them all!"

COMMENTARY
BY GREGORY BOYD

Gregory Boyd became the artistic director of the Alley Theatre in 1989. During his tenure, the Alley has risen in national and international prominence, winning the 1996 Tony Award. Mr. Boyd has directed more than twenty Alley productions, including The Greeks, Cyrano de Bergerac, In the Jungle of Cities, Jekyll & Hyde *(premiere),* The Three Sisters, The Food Chain, Svengali *(premiere) and* Measure for Measure. *He has directed theatre and opera across America, including eleven seasons at Williamstown as director and actor, and he has been on the faculties of Carnegie Mellon, Williams, and the University of North Carolina.*

Nikos was a great *connoisseur* of acting.

I mean, that in addition to his skill as director, and his genius as teacher, impresario, and producer, he knew and understood — better than anybody, I think — what made good acting "work" and what made the experience of being in the room with great acting ineffable.

I invited him over one night and we watched sequences from some of my favorite film performances (Olivier in *The Entertainer,* Michael Redgrave in *Dead of Night* and *The Browning Version*, and both knights together in their *Uncle Vanya*.) And his excitement of and love for what he called the "inner promise" — of having "something more to do" than what is shown, was much in evidence in the way he spoke about the two actors. "Olivier's an iceberg" he said — "nine-tenths below the surface." This I thought an astonishing thing to say about who I had always considered a wonderfully "showy" performer. Then we talked about what Olivier actually "did" as the character — all the wonderful business and behavior and the unexpected readings — and *then* what immense material all that "covered up."

I would watch him watch actors, and I realized that he watched them either "coldly" — that is, analytically — or with great ardor and "heat" — going through the emotion of the work himself with them. Never tepidly, never politely. Like an orchestra conductor, he could have a very wound-up and intimate and passionate relationship with the acting and also be able to pinpoint a problem of technique.

The eleven seasons I spent at Williamstown were witness to some great performances. I think particularly of Blythe Danner in *Sea Gull* and *Three Sisters* and *Ring Round the Moon* and *Enemies*, and Dwight Schultz in *Idiot's Delight* and Roberta Maxwell as Electra — all actors who possess abundantly the qualities Nikos reveres here — an "edge" and a physical and emotional courage and the ability to "synthesize" the scene onstage, in performance — and keep it alive and "unfinished." We would talk about the effect I felt from these performances and he would laugh at my enthusiasm for them. "You like this moment or that moment because you are an actor! But you should try to imagine what the audience sees and feels. It's easy for us to admire the work of actors we know and love — but that love and admiration has to be strict and kept in balance. We cannot allow ourselves, or the actor, to get away with less than they are capable of — and *never* to 'set' the performance."

"All good actors are unfinished actors," he says here. The challenge is to never be finished. Very naked work.

Part Six
Toward Mastery

> ...We two are monsters but with this difference between us. Out of the passion and torment of my existence, I have created a thing that I can unveil, a sculpture, almost heroic, that I can unveil, which is true!
>
> Princess, Sweet Bird of Youth
Tennessee Williams

SHARPENING TECHNIQUE

The actors have performed a scene from Harold Pinter's Betrayal. *Nikos now takes work that is more advanced and fine-tunes it specifically to the playwright and to each actor. Now that the acting problems have diminished, he talks about the different techniques necessary to approach specific writers' work.*

NIKOS: Really wonderful. I think you both did very good work. I mean, it's the kind of acting we want to pay to see and that is rare! Ellie, I've seen you several times now, and I just thought there were terrific things in the way you used yourself, and in the openness and specificity of the love relationship between the two of you. And Bill, I have never before seen you have that much authority. You had a quiet, understated authority that a lot of guys, you know, in movies have built very good careers on! You both were so attractive up there, and I don't mean just how you looked, but attractive in how you dealt with your needs. You both have come a long way and you should feel very proud of yourselves.

Except, Bill, sometimes the scene was not about an effort. It was about an accomplishment. It became vignettes about the problem and vignettes about the love and vignettes about the hurt, and so occasionally, the bottom fell out. The bottom falls out of any scene when the actor deals not with an *attempt*, but with a *realization*. Your work was very interesting, there was a great deal of freedom and you played well with each other, but sometimes the work was about kissing rather than an effort to kiss, an effort to hug, an effort to deal with one thing because of the inability to deal with something else. Many times you were reaching moments of acceptance of what was happening, and because of that the scene occasionally became glib.

In a way, you really made yourself like — things — up there. Like two happy-go-lucky guys. So you didn't need anything. It was as if you can just go kiss each other, everything will be okay overnight. But, in the scene, everything is not okay. So it is making an *attempt* at reaching, it is making an *attempt* at loving, it is making an *attempt* at being close together, it is making an *attempt* at forgetting, not achieving these things, but *attempting* to achieve them. The effort in the scene was gone, and the effort is essential no matter what the interpretation is, for any kind of acting.

If your interpretation is "I love this person," it is not interesting to deal with the love. What's interesting is to deal with is the fact that "I love him but I cannot love him." What's interesting is, "I'll attempt not to love him." As Masha says in *The Sea Gull:* "I've decided, I'll tear this love out of my heart." Or, if your interpretation is "I don't love this person," you play "I don't love him but I wish I could love him."

For this material, for Pinter, I think it is wonderful if you allow the silent moments to deal away from the verbal moments in the scene. There is a play going on in the pauses and a play going on in the lines. And on a peculiar level these two plays should not meet. Because if they meet, you are doing verbally what you have already done visually. It is material where the subtext and text don't exist together. And I thought you tried to make these things come in together. Your inner life was wonderful, Bill, but I just think you decided to fling the life before anybody asked for it, or worked hard to get it. And therefore your inner life became an Alka-seltzer with your reality, rather than something you had deep within you. So that in the audience we would say, "He has so much more underneath that he isn't showing."

But again, it was the kind of work we want and that is taken seriously, and you can really see that they did not "deliver" lines, they invested them with life and that is what, at the end of the day, really counts for a lot. Good life, wonderful acting.

TELLING THE STORY

Often actors worked on directed scenes in class. In this unidentified scene, Nikos talks about the director's point of view in terms of the "street" the director chooses to go down and techniques for matching the actors' sensibilities to the director's images.

NIKOS: I'm thinking this is a wonderful scene to give to three different groups of actors and tell one group to play it as a comedy, and another group as a tragedy, and another as a melodrama or farce or whatever. Because it can go in any direction. And I think that was the problem, which has to do with your point of view toward the scene. Brad had a line — "I love your earrings." But it was neither Noël Coward, as in "I love telling you that I love your earrings;" nor was it Sam Shepard, as in "I'm so addicted to you, I love your earrings." Or Chekhov, as in "I love you but I don't know how to tell you, so instead I say I love your earrings." I think directing is going through and telling the actors what kind of world they are in. I'm talking about their perceptions and their feelings about the world they are dealing with and what things mean in that world.

First, I feel that any two characters have to connect with an event. And that, directorally, your obligation is to make that event clear, and to make them part of one world, even though, possibly, they deal with the event differently. I just kept trying to identify, when somebody said "Remember our lives," if that was something good or bad, or if they remembered it with some kind of sexual desire or remembered all the miseries, and how when somebody says "remember" it sparks a reference in the other. But here it was like somebody said, (*Flippantly:*) "Remember!" and the other person goes (*Low, sad, mumbling:*) "Yeah, I remember." It's not that they have to use the same tone, it's about having a point of view about the gravity of the events that is similar. If that's there, even if one person laughs at the event and the other person cries at the event, we can still see the same kind of event. I don't think they were seeing matching images about the events, and if they don't have that, you're in trouble.

You can make a play a melodrama by emphasizing lines two, four, six, and eight; you can make it a comedy by emphasizing lines one, four, and seven, you can make it absurdist by taking lines five, eleven, and twenty. What I'm saying is not so much about the traditional idea of making something a comedy or making something a drama, but about the actors having the same sources for their particular event. Because they didn't have the same sources it was hard for us to get the event. I kept trying to figure it out. I kept saying to myself: "I wonder if this is supposed to be funny?" And then: "No, no, it's serious."

It was as if you were two strangers in a gallery looking at a painting and then "Oh!" — you bump into each other. But if the one person says (*Dramatically, seriously:*) "It's you," and the other person (*Screaming, giddy:*) "Oh, it's you!" — forget it, you can't connect to the scene. Because then the serious person would have to say to the giddy person: "What happened to you? You've changed."

Look. You go back and remember a day. You say: "Well, let me tell you what I did today." Then you might say, "Well, at 10:00 I did this, at 12:00 I did this, at 3:00 I did this and at 5:00 I did this. That's one kind of a day. But if you say, at 11:30 I did this, at 12:15 I did this, at 3:35 I did this, that's another kind of a day. You remember a day the way you remember a play: about the sort of things directorally you pick to emphasize or to make sense of.

Because this was a directed scene, I tried to find out what you picked to emphasize. It certainly couldn't have been the love. It certainly couldn't have been the past. It certainly couldn't have be the husband, it certainly couldn't have been his lust. I kept trying to find out what was the new thing that the words didn't tell us that you were trying to tell us with this scene. Directorally I've done that by giving people a scene to direct from *The Visit* and see what they find. Or, God knows, that's the great reason for doing the Chekhovs over and over and over again. The first time I did *Sea Gull*, I was fascinated with Constantin; the second time I was fascinated with Arkadina; the third time, Nina. And then you see everything from their point of view, which is not what Chekhov has done in the play, but because you are at a certain stage in the work you need to do that. You have your point of view, then every time one of the characters says "Constantin's silly" you make that person say it in such a way that nobody else is going to believe it. Even when you don't think about interpretations, still, that's your own version of it. But here, their rhythms were so different and their sense of the event was so different that I had no idea what your version was, Robert. So it became like a Feydeau that backfired: actors in search of a style.

THE DIRECTOR: We spent a great deal of time trying to give it a sense of mystery —

NIKOS: I think the most interesting thing directorally is to tell them the story, you know what I mean?

THE DIRECTOR: I'm not sure.

NIKOS: Anya in *The Cherry Orchard* comes home in the first scene, right? You can say to the actress playing Anya, "You enter the house, you look at the walls, there's forty paintings, there are people serving you, there is a marvelous ceiling, there is a butler coming in to take your coat, and through the windows you see a glorious light from the cherry orchard — now play the scene." Or you can say, "You have traveled for days, you are very tired, you're dirty, you're dying to go to sleep. You have moved away from all this fancy world, you are anxious to go to the bathroom, you have not eaten and you're starving to death, you don't know what to do." Now all of that is there in the first act of *Cherry Orchard*, but it all depends on what you tell your people.

ACTOR: Which version…

NIKOS: Absolutely right! If it's the first version, Anya would say (*With a joyful cry:*) "I'm so sleepy!" and she would be playing "But I can't sleep because I'm looking at the light from these cherry trees!" If it's the second version she says "I'm so sleepy" and she wants to go to bed. You know what I'm saying? Because, you see, plays don't *discover* themselves directorally. I mean, I think the idea of people saying "Let's rehearse for six months because we're going to discover it" is — (*Nikos lets out a yell:*) AAAAAHHHHH — NO! You can fill it with meaning, because that's where you need the time. But you're not going to really discover it.

If you have the story you want to tell, you will be able to adjust slowly to do the kind of work that's important for actors and directors, because then you're trying to find the nuances of certain undiscoverable things. And then time is important, because the more time you have the richer it can become, the texture. But you don't spend the time doing a hundred different versions. Now, out of the hundred possible ways you might try to find out which six or seven ways are more possible. But I'm telling you, if you go down one street you discover one thing, if you go another street you will discover something else completely. So it's much better to choose which street, and then start to work, rather than making the work about going down all different streets. Choose one street, but then take the time to look at little bit here, to look there, to peer in this doorway, and go down that back alley. You don't want to force it, which is what we do when we don't have enough rehearsal time, we hit the end of the street, and lose all the exciting things which are happening along the way — but first you've got to choose the kind of street you're going to go down.

MAKING SKETCHES

In this scene from Ashes *by David Rudkin, Nikos talks about the conditions the actor needs to create within himself in order to sustain the work — from a scene in class to a long run in a play. Developing a lack of reverence as well as keeping each performance "unfinished" are discussed, along with the necessity for the actor in any scene to play against the text.* Ashes *is about two people who are trying to conceive a child and the agony of their failure to do so. But the critique here is less about the specifics of the play than it is about a specific technique for working on any confrontational scene.*

NIKOS: Joan, your best moment in the scene was when the prop didn't work for you, that was wonderful. That's exactly how good acting comes out of good directing: The director sets something in the right way, but shifts it away from the actor. As a director, give an actor a wrapped package and say, "Just open it very nicely and easily," but then tie the strings very tight, so the actor has to make an effort.

In the same way, I would have felt much better, Sheila, (*Nikos is addressing the director of the scene:*) if in the first part of the scene the actors had made much more of an effort to make the relationship work. If you had tried to give much more, Michael, and then allowed yourself to feel the frustration, if you make a huge effort for things to go your way and then life catches up with you in just the opposite way, it's much more exciting for you as an actor than knowing in advance that this is going to be a confrontational scene.

Although I felt the love and warmth between you, you needed to make a very definite attempt to play against what is written, which is, of course, an argument. For your part, Joan, if you hadn't made the words so abrupt, and if you had assumed you were going into a love scene rather than a confrontation, it would be so much more spine-chilling for us and more devastating for you as an actress. I guess I'm saying that it would be much more interesting if the life of the scene were constantly going against your feelings, instead of your feelings mirroring the lines.

It's always more interesting in acting if you play against the inevitability of what the playwright gives you or challenge what the playwright gives you with your own expectations. And then, in the middle of it, you *find* yourself in the scene the playwright has written. It sort of a cliché, but there's nothing like a love scene starting out of a quarrel. It's a very simple thing, good playwrights do it. If you start a love scene lovingly, most of the time you're in trouble.

This scene is an argument and I felt that it started much too much from a lack of communication — not through your attitude, but through your use of tempo, through using a precise, no-nonsense tempo in the delivery of the lines. It's always much better for you as actors to deal with weakness, vulnerability, or effort that cannot possibly succeed, than with precision. That's why the last part of the scene was so moving for you and for us, because you were trying, making the effort to play a different scene from the one that was written.

In acting terms — not for us but for you — it makes much more sense if you do not think from the beginning that the scene is about a disaster, a confrontation. Think of things as actors to try that the play will never let you get to, but nonetheless your heart or your imagination compels you to try, rather than making choices that will succeed because of the inevitability of the scene itself. If you succeed too easily in realizing the scene as written, than we get a scene that seems spelled out with alphabet blocks.

ACTRESS: I know you hate to hear what we were going to do but I'm going to say it anyway. I felt like in rehearsal we went so much slower — just now I felt like the scene got out of my hands, sped up — that made me very nervous.

NIKOS: Well, let me suggest something. Always have dead moments in a scene. Directorally, I always try to give actors moments away from the audience. Say maybe, going to the bar to fix a drink, or looking upstage at a painting, not because the business is needed, but because that is a time for the actor to catch up, to come back to himself and his objectives. If as an actor you can 'drop out' for a moment, you have the chance to say to yourself, "What the hell am I doing?" It's a moment like a string around your finger reminding you of what you want to do.

So to make it safe for yourself — of course, it's never really safe, which is wonderful — but to make it a little safer, always give yourself a few moments here and there when you are not constantly on the spot. It's wonderful how actors who have worked with each other for a while know just how long to touch each other in order to reach each other. It's the perfect example of using craft for the sake of art, and giving yourself a sort of time-out on stage works in the same way.

Now, Michael, I was lost in your long speech. Although it came out accidentally, which was wonderful, it occurred to me that in real life, when people get really involved in speeches like that, something hidden within them comes out about why the story was told. You start telling a story and then you discover that something else, unexpectedly, takes over. That you're not really telling what you thought you would, or you're revealing more than you ever intended. This happens all the time to us in everyday conversation, think about it. But here, I didn't think anything you didn't expect to say or to feel took over during that speech.

THE ACTOR: I had rehearsed it in order to try to let it register at a certain point that the character can't feel. What upsets me so much about the two scenes I've done in this class, is that stuff just runs away and I really don't take the time to allow things to happen, I just let it run away. I don't take time — it's like a racehorse — I can't seem to…

NIKOS: Get it back.

THE ACTOR: Yes.

NIKOS: But how much do you do, how many of those do you do, regularly?

THE ACTOR: I'm sorry, I don't follow you.

NIKOS: How many scenes do you do, like in a month?

THE ACTOR: Well, one.

NIKOS: So why should you really assume it's *not* going to run away from you?

(*Much laughter from the class. Nikos cuts it off in his usual way.*) AAAAH-HHHH! You know what I mean? It's like me saying I'm going out there and jogging four miles today. Forget it, it's not going to happen! Unless you're doing it regularly, unless you're constantly doing it, it's not going to happen, so why do you expect it will? That's why people rehearse; people are not rehearsing for things to go right, people are rehearsing for all the things that are going to go wrong! If you really assume that the one time you go up there in a month you're going to hit it right, you'll worry yourself to death because the odds of hitting it are really not very good. You did remarkably well considering you do one scene a month.

That is the whole purpose of working constantly. I can understand your impatience, but it's a thing about time. That's why when Thornton Wilder was asked "Who's your best friend?" he said: "The wastepaper basket!" When you look through all the notebooks of Michelangelo, or da Vinci, or Picasso, there's a hell of a lot of pieces of paper, yet in between you still imagine that for each sketch, at least ten sketches were torn out.

You're coming in to do a sketch, just one quick sketch in front of everyone, right? The point is, you have to create for yourself — and that is why we are here — you have to create the conditions to go up there and do the work with much less reverence and much less expectation. Accept that automatically things happen, and at the end you don't say ponder over your sketch wondering why it's not quite right but you just take a quick look and say, "Oh, yeah, I messed it up," or even, really, you don't remember it. Because you're on to the next one.

When the time comes that you go out of a performance and you don't remember if it was good or if it was bad, then you know you're working. If you really, really worry, saying "This is good," or "This is bad," just forget it, screw it. I mean, it's just not worth it or even that interesting! There have to be many more interesting things for you to do, as a person, as Michael. You can have a drink, a meal, you can go on a trip, see nature, why should you go through this agony? Unless of course you get your kicks that way!

Don't worry if something goes wrong or right. If you worry about it, it's going to go wrong. You know? Do it kind of as part of your existence. Next Thursday it doesn't work, the Friday after that it works. Some people need to do twenty a year, some need three. The other day I talked to — I won't say who — but a brilliant actress, and she said "I don't want to appear again in New York," and I said "What do you mean? You're a major actress in the American theater!" She said: "No, I won't." Because five or six years ago she got a very bad review, this upset her, so she won't come back. So the first time she comes back, she's going to screw up no matter what she does. Because there's not going to be that sense of throwing the work away. It's going to matter.

Yes, you're right, you did speed it up. It did get away from you, but this time, at least, compared to the last, there was less imposition and doubt in you. So if within two or three weeks rehearsing only a few hours, that much can happen, think what can happen if you're working the regular eighty-hour week! For two or three hundred weeks!

ACTOR: Yes, I see. It would be nice to be — working at Williamstown. To be able to say, "See you in the morning."

NIKOS: (*Thrown off.*) Yeah, exactly.

(*The class laughs.*)

ACTOR: Just kidding. No, I mean, I auditioned for the Second Company* last week.

NIKOS: (*After a pause:*) Aha. (*He is on the spot.*)

(*More laughter from the class.*)

NIKOS: (*Laughing uncomfortably:*) AAAAHHHH... Anyway. I think what happens in that last speech in the writing, and I say this without ever having worked on this material, is that all of a sudden that character moves into his own world. And what is that world? It's got to be an excursion into something about your own life, or how you imagine your life. Only you know what that is. You might either find something or put something in. Either discover it in the material or invent it from your own life. But either way, you didn't deal enough with that secret world, which, if you were playing eight shows a week, would keep it from being boring for you. Also, a couple of times Michael, I felt you were making more of a panic than was necessary — in the second part you took your time more, you were not so afraid of your emotional world so you had less need to exaggerate it.

Joan, don't package it. You package it well, but you package it. You should really have much more unfinished life on stage. Start with threads and colors you're never going to use. And I know, easier said than done. But you can afford to be a little more eccentric, a little more mischievous. You must learn as an actress to use what I call emotional parenthetical sentences. You must start something and then drop it, and you must cultivate the instinct to do that in yourself.

---

*The Williamstown Theatre Festival's Second Company was often made up of Nikos' students. Nikos probably wasn't present for the initial audition, but eventually he would be at the final callbacks.

THE ACTRESS: Except when I did Miss Julie, you said I was dropping threads too much.

NIKOS: I'm not sure that was the same thing. I meant you were finishing certain tasks — you'd drop the love for him or the need for him and kept picking up different things. Even that had a certain clarity, too much clarity. Instead, what I'm saying is, keep the underlying need consistent, and then bring other colors that come from your private world into it. Need him throughout the scene and weave the threads of your personal idiosyncracies through that need. When you say a line you tend to finish it where the playwright gives you a period, rather than saying the line you're given but wanting to go on and on and on — except the playwright doesn't give you that many lines.

Your audience is very bright, they can read the play and get it. They don't need you to clarify it for them. They need you to filter it through whatever is maladjusted or unfinished or unsaid in you in order for the performance to be interesting and alive. Look, play that scene every day for three weeks instead of once and you'll be dying to entertain yourself, forget the audience, you'll be dying to keep yourself interested. Actors only ever go wrong in long runs because they haven't found that unfinished part of themselves to filter through whatever role they're playing every night. Find that one unfinished thing in you, that is informed by the circumstances of the play and you'll never go wrong.

PLAYING WITH SHAW

> *At the end of* Mrs. Warren's Profession *by George Bernard Shaw, Vivie tells her mother that she will never see her again. Mrs. Warren, whose prostitution business has provided her daughter with a very good life, is astounded by Vivie's rejection. Vivie makes it clear that she has understood and forgiven her mother for her running a house of prostitution, but not for her hypocrisy — living one way and pretending to the world that she lives another. In this climatic scene, Vivie declares her intention to break with her mother and make her way on her own. As the actors in the scene are advanced, Nikos focuses specifically on the challenges inherent to Shaw.*

NIKOS: What's marvelous in any Shaw play is that no matter what position, no matter what point of view a character takes — politically, emotionally, morally — every position is, on its own, interesting and alive and exciting. A really perfect production of a George Bernard Shaw play would consist of twelve people who are exactly like Shaw. Ideally, when you direct Shaw, you should think of having many little George Bernard Shaws all over the stage all fighting and loving and dealing with each other! Because basically, Shaw is a man arguing with himself. Because he's so educated and so brilliant, all these different aspects of his nature come out in the point of view of each one of the characters. Therefore, all the characters have a *use* for each other. Nobody in Shaw ever has no *use* for the other person they are on stage with. And in this scene, Vivie and Mrs. Warren have a great *use* for each other.

You both got very negative with the roles and that is wrong. You made it so much of a fight against each other that I lost the positive way of dealing with these particular problems. I'm not saying you dismissed each other but you really did not have much use for each other. You were attacking each other rather than saying to yourself "How interested I am in her philosophy…but I have something else in my mind that is even more interesting and knowledgeable than that!" In Shaw, any topic has two equally interesting, equally relevant, equally challenging points of view — not one wrong point of view and one right point of view. For example, that great argument Ellie makes in *Heartbreak House* (*Nikos paraphrases the following speech:*)

> *A soul is a very expensive thing to keep…it eats music and pictures and books and mountains and lakes and beautiful things to wear and nice people to be with. In this country you can't have them without lots of money: that is why our souls are so horribly starved.*

Right there is the wonderful paradox of Shaw. I mean, here he is relating something very spiritual, the ultimate health of the soul, to something very materialistic, having lots of money. Think of it! And in a way, Shaw's philosophy of life is very opposed to the sort of mentality we have now, in our group-therapy society, which is: "It doesn't matter who you are, you're somebody anyway." It's part of the whole democracy thing, one man/one vote! Now Shaw didn't feel that way, obviously. Shaw felt people needed to *earn* their value.

When you got upset by the argument in the scene, Isabelle, you dealt the fact that your character doesn't want to be a daughter and doesn't want to be a wife. That is not what Shaw wants because that is very negative. In this modern world we live in we assume that mothers and fathers are out to get us, that we are constantly being criticized and attacked. We are used to fighting against things rather than for things. Shaw fights *for* things. He doesn't have Vivie say, "Mother, you are attacking me and you are impossible." He has her say, very openly and positively, "Sure, Mother, this is very possible and that is very possible, but I have another life which is more interesting, which is, you know, more *me*."

Shaw felt that there is something about your center, or about each character's center, that in its essence is tremendously interesting, alive and exciting. And each of his characters recognizes this in each other. So it is never about trying to attack the other person. And when it seems like the other person gets attacked, it's not that the other person gets attacked, but what that person *stands for* that is attacked. It is driven by intelligence rather than emotion, it's about the kind of people who have sufficient intelligence to respond to challenges in a highly articulate way. And it is definitely not about anybody quieting anybody else's style. It is not a case where individual conflict and obstacles are bad, and painful, and to be avoided. It is a case where conflicts and problems between people are welcomed and embraced. Because in Shaw, these are the things that bring the best out in you.

It's like I said — I mean, we are all so very aware and sensitive in our interactions at this point in time that when something is said, the other person often assumes it's a criticism rather than a very definite statement. So when Vivie talks about making about money, for example, it is not a criticism of her mother, it is not a negative statement, it is just a very definite statement that she is making about her independence. It is a positive statement about one's own life force, one's own essence, rather than a criticism of someone else's.

In the production I recently saw here in New York, they tried to make it all very tearful, and that is difficult when the speeches are that long. It really is. Now, when does a playwright write a long speech? A playwright writes a long speech when he delights in making more than just a functional statement. When it's not emotional. A long speech doesn't exist for somebody to say "No, no, no," over and over! The force behind Shaw's long speeches is not the characters saying "No, no, no," to each other. Instead, the character says, "I will now talk for a long time to tell you why your view of life is not as interesting as something else." In all the long speeches, Shaw's characters say to each other: "What you're saying is fascinating, but I also have some new wisdom to add to it." I mean, it's interesting, it's English, but there's something the same in a lot of the Russian plays. There is no diminishing of the other's point of view. In Russian plays, of course, they go back and forth about feelings and in Shaw they do it about ideas. In Shaw, people debate, passionately debate, ideas. And because they live through those ideas, these debates then also become personal and emotional.

But even if it were not Shaw, the two of you did not have much *use* for each other which is always very wrong for two people on stage together. You see, you've got to love the other person. I've said many times, even in the bullfight, the bullfighter loves the bull. Otherwise you cannot have acting. You dealt with what was separating you in the scene rather than what keeps you together. But why would somebody deliver a page-long speech if it's about separation? Why would somebody listen to a page-long speech? When the other person was talking, both of you were playing a subtext, and that subtext was "No, no, no." But saying "no," does not encourage the other person to go on with her speech. Your task as actors in this material is to encourage the other person to go on talking. And then you will find that these long, long speeches, when said in a very positive way, become about awareness.

Through listening to and making these speeches, the characters make discoveries about themselves, about the fact that perhaps there is something else more possible, more alive.

As I said, in a scene like this, you've got to find a reason, you've got to find the reason *why* you are on stage together. What *use* you have for the other character. And I use the word *use* as something great and healthy. Not in terms of, again, what we have now — "He's using me, she's using me" — not in a derogatory way. I'm using it terms of *a need based on past knowledge*, where in effect, being "used" is great. I mean, there's nothing wrong with people using people once a relationship is created, everybody does it! And that's what Shaw is writing about, a relationship. And then this relationship reaches a point where the most essential part of you — the sense of what keeps you going — no longer coincides with the sense of what keeps her going.

There is no judgement in Shaw and there should not be in your acting about who is wrong and who is right. Otherwise this play and this scene about a mother who is a prostitute and a daughter who is trying to break away would become a morality play, a morality issue, and clearly that is not what Shaw has in mind. Look at the shape of the scene — it is a debate, not an argument. If it were a morality issue, it would be just the opposite. Besides Shaw is brilliant and as we all know, by watching, you know, fanatics and evangelical speakers and right-wing politicians, people who make issues out of morality are not very bright.

I thought you were both very honest and very sincere but I kept saying to myself, why don't they speak in shorter sentences since they have no *use* for each other? And, consequently, you have no use for yourselves. You were not — unfolding — discovering with your lines, such as: "This is what I think, and I think this and I think that and let me tell you!" You were not, through the conflict and confrontation and debate, actively finding your own values, finding the excitement of being where you are and who you are. Instead you made it all about dismissing where the other person is. You kept dismissing each other's position, and therefore you had not as much respect as you should have for your opponent, for the person who is on the same stage with you.

Find always in Shaw what is positive, what keeps you together, what makes it exciting for you to be on the same stage, and unfold these ideas not as things you already knew but things you are finding out as you speak. And then, eventually, when Vivie asks to shake her mother's hand at the end, that will come as a big surprise to both of you. I thought your conviction was wonderful, but your conviction didn't add up to the relationship between them. It was about two people who really despised each other rather than about a loving mother and a loving daughter who say to each other, "Look, understand me, this is what the world is all about." Or: "I love you, but this is not what the world is all about."

It's almost as if all of Shaw's characters are saying: "Let's come together every Thursday night and debate about life!" When you find the delight in the debate, you'll also find out that the scene could take more time and there would be no problem with that, because the scene could be more specific. Then it would be wonderful because what we all would want to do is come back every Thursday night and watch you argue and watch you debate. That's the difference between Shaw and somebody else, you know, a lesser playwright. With a lesser playwright it is agonizing and draining watching characters being involved with each other — like the way we feel when we watch those people on a soap opera! You know, there are all these sighs. (*Nikos talks in a labored, exhausted way.*) Like, "Everything I have to say to you and everything you say to me we wish we were not and we wish we did not have to have this scene with each other because relating is just so damn difficult!" Whereas with Shaw we feel that these people love to be dealing with each other, love to be *involved*. And we love to be there every day watching them.

ACTRESS: I think maybe we did better before we started, quote unquote, "acting." When we didn't feel an obligation to act.

NIKOS: Well, Shaw said: "Please don't act these plays!" Basically what Shaw says is that every time people started adding acting to his lines, he was in trouble. Now, obviously what he meant by "acting" was making it all about subtext rather than text.

ACTRESS: We both kept thinking something was missing. We kept talking about that in rehearsal, and I think it's just not knowing what to do with Shaw, how to approach it.

NIKOS: But as I say, even if it were not Shaw, the idea is that twenty percent of your character should be in Vivie and the other way around. No good playwright has ever a scene where the two people are totally different. A percentage of each of them exists in the other person, that's why they can talk. Especially in a play like this where there are no heros or villains, protagonists or antagonists, where in effect everybody represents a very interesting point of view.

We don't want to see her, the mother, through the eyes of the daughter more than we want to see the daughter through the eyes of the mother. We've got to see you in your own world, we've got to see those two worlds, both for the audience and for yourselves. Now, if I was playing Mrs. Warren to your Vivie, I would feel too upset to share my point of view with you, because you were so emotionally undone that for Mrs. Warren to attack your position would be cruel. And, Mrs. Warren, because you were passing judgement on the nature of your lines about the money and the house of prostitution, sometimes it felt almost like you had no feeling about your own life. You were making the character something of a cynic or an opportunist and that is not the case. Mrs. Warren doesn't condemn her own life, it is a life she loves and has chosen and has served her well! And it comes in as big surprise to her that her daughter doesn't cherish the same things she does.

I guess what I'm saying is, watch it so that you don't make so many judgements, leave your judgements outside, because Shaw doesn't judge. Shaw doesn't condemn either of them, he wants to hear each point of view, and he wants us to hear it and he wants us to perceive each point of view equally. And in hearing these points of view the characters make perceptions about their own lives, through which we make perceptions about our own lives. Not judgements about our lives. *Perceptions.*

PUTTING IT TOGETHER

Nikos' advanced class at Yale focused all year on a production of Uncle Vanya, *and the following critique is of the whole of Act II. It is a sort of tour-de-force commentary on the art of acting, and even though Nikos is responding to the specificity of Chekhov, the gist of what he is saying can be applied to any playwright and any kind of acting: stage or film. It would help the reader enormously to read (or re-read) Act II of* Uncle Vanya *in order to gain understanding in context. I have also provided the following synopsis.*

SYNOPSIS OF UNCLE VANYA, ACT II

Act Two begins late on a stormy night in the dining room of the Professor's (Serebrayakov's) country house. Serebrayakov, ill, has trouble sleeping. Yelena, his young wife, sits and tries to comfort him but he rails against the difficulty of growing old and the pain he has from gout. Eventually Sonya, Serbrayakov's daughter, and Vanya, the brother of his first wife, come in to take their turns with him. Irascible, the Professor refuses to see Astrov, the doctor he requested. Finally Marina, the old servant, convinces him to go to bed.

Yelena voices her frustration about the way the family lives; Vanya, who has been drinking, confesses his love for her. Exasperated, Yelena leaves the room. Left alone, Vanya speaks of his longing for love and the mistakes he feels he's made in his life, especially in idolizing and working for his brother-in-law, Serebrayakov.

Astrov, who has also been drinking, comes in. He and Vanya talk circumspectly about their attraction to Yelena as Telyegin, a servant, plays the guitar. Astrov goes to get another drink; Sonya reappears and as she chastises her uncle for drinking, he is struck by her resemblance to his late sister, Sonya's mother. He leaves the room in tears.

Sonya calls Astrov in and begs him not to let Vanya drink. She gives Astrov some food and he talks about his disgust with Russian life, his lack of satisfaction with his private life, the rigors of his duties as a country doctor — and Yelena's beauty. Sonya implores him to stop drinking, extols his virtues, and then speaks covertly of her love for him. He suggests he cannot return such a love and quickly exits.

Alone, Sonya expresses both her happiness in loving Astrov and her despair that she is not beautiful. Yelena comes in, acknowledges the uneasiness between them, and insists they become friends again. They drink a toast to their friendship, and Sonya, crying, confesses her love for Astrov. Yelena speaks at some length about Astrov's talents and the hardships of his life as a country doctor and admits to Sonya that she is "very, very unhappy." At the end of the scene Yelena wants to play the piano, something she hasn't done in a long while. She sends Sonya to go to Serebrayakov to ask if she may. The act ends with Sonya reappearing and telling Yelena, "He says no."

NIKOS: Okay, guys, I will talk initially about the overall picture and then I'll move to each specific scene.

First of all, I think all of you kept score of what you were doing on stage. You were like children in a sandbox, saying "This is a moment about laughter." "This is a moment about a piano." "This is a moment about grapes." All of which is true, but in effect we were getting the detail before we were getting the life of the detail. Like the way medieval painters have someone like St. Nicholas carrying a little ball. You look at the ball and say: "Aha! He loves sailors!" You don't get to see it from the faces, you don't get to see it from the deeds, you see it from the *attributes* they gave.

In the same way, your behavior many times turned into attributes. The behavior turned into attributes because it was bound up with such a sense of invention, either on the part of the actor or director. It was very clearly pointed up that: This moment is about two people getting drunk; this is moment is about somebody holding a bottle. It's like you were all constantly saying: "This is something important." "This is something precious." "This is something telling." The details became "telling" rather than casually thrown in. So it became a scene about people inventing rather than about people discovering.

In essence it's what I've been saying about Picasso. Picasso could paint with a stick in the sand, as well as with a brush on a canvas. Sometime or another, the work has to become accidental. So that all those things that either the director or the actors put in disappear — how they happen disappears and they happen accidentally. So you do not remember the moments of behavior in their exactness or in sequence but you remember their essence, you remember them in your imagination.

It's really wonderful when someone comes up to me about a play that I've directed and says, "Oh, how wonderful she was! She did this and this, and the way she comes down the staircase!" And a little while later, you think "Wait — there was not a staircase!" Or: "There were a lot of staircases, but she never came down one!" That is what imagination has to do in the theater. With the good actors that you trust, you almost think they did something that they did not. Moments in the theater have become legendary that never really happened! You never want to say, "Sweetheart, you never did that! Everybody just *assumes* you did that in a performance!" In Williamstown we keep doing shows that we've done before and the new actor will come to me and say, "Oh, I hear the last time you did this play so and so did this and that." And everyone agrees and then I think back: "No, she never did that!" It's because something in the performance led to certain assumptions. What's that line about — education is what remains known of what remains of education — it's that kind of thing.

What really happens is, once the details become forgotten they become much more interesting. Because then you find out that your activity becomes an *inevitable* way for you to behave, rather than coming out of a conscious decision about how you will behave up there. So the sixty-three little things that one puts in a scene becomes one, and the actor and the director and the audience never know where the one begins and the other ends.

Now, when you make your behavior into "symbols" or "attributes" that are so clearly defined, this not only causes the process to get lost but it also sterilizes you vocally. I thought that a lot of you were putting in very definite strokes with your voice. I would not have gotten what scenes were about if I'd just been listening to you and not able to see you. I got the scenes physically but not vocally. When we were doing Pinter's *Old Times*, Elizabeth Smith, who is a brilliant voice teacher, said "Well, you're never going to solve it because all the lights are on." And somebody said: "What?" She said: "All the lights are on. Turn off the lights so the actors can't see each other, so they have to do the whole damn play by just using their voices. That's all they have to depend on. They can go through the moves, they can do all the behavior, but it's not in someone looking in the eyes, the play is in the voices."

You were shortchanging your voices many times. Your voices didn't have either the desperation or the enjoyment. They did not have the connection of, (*Long, drawn-out, plaintively:*) "Why——?" It is more interesting if it is (*Again, drawn out, longingly:*) "Why——" than if it is (*Short, staccato:*) "Why." Why is this? Because "why" is a *searching* word, right? And your voices should mirror that. This is why it's tough occasionally in translations, because people cannot find the equivalent sound to the original one. So the meaning comes in as *text* rather than as a sound in a language. Which is wrong because many times the feeling of the word is the sound of the word. Language obviously is "sounds" as much as is it "meaning." Somebody like Tennessee Williams picks up long sentences as much for the way they fall on the ear as for what they mean.

The things you pick up to do in Chekhov, your acting tasks, should never be as appropriate as they were now. Your behavior was really too appropriate. Your choices were absolutely right, absolutely literal, the sort of things which makes an audience kind of relax, because everybody "gets" everything. Then the things you do become like a simultaneous translation, really. And although sometimes these things were interesting and alive, although you were having a great deal of fun, even though the things the director gave you created a great deal of freedom, they were too appropriate.

Don't assume, consciously or subconsciously, that everything gets solved in every moment. When you have fourteen tasks up there, when you have fourteen things working for you, make them springboards for the life of the scene rather than guideposts. Make the tasks things that bounce you up and down and make you do other things that you don't know you are going to do. Rather than using the tasks as "If I do that, it means I'm happy," "If I do this, it means I'm worried." In essence sometimes some of you seemed dubbed in the scene, you seemed dubbed because a problem had been solved before the text came in, and the problem was solved by a very interesting and colorful visual image. As I said, it's like the painters who used attributes to tell the story. You invented behavior which then became symbolic of something else. And all this richness of detail sometimes became an end in itself instead of being used as possibilities to stimulate you. The ideal kind of work between a director and an actor is not discovering that thing that tells the story, but discovering those things that cultivate the emotional world of the actor to become more open and more free. We've somehow got to be able to differentiate between these things.

ACTRESS: So that it's not so literal?

NIKOS: No, no, it's not necessarily that. I mean it's fascinating, a lot of times in movies a lot of the work is literal, the director puts in very literal things to tell the audience what it's all about. It's okay if it's literal as long as it's creating the conditions for the actor to respond. What I'm saying is that definition has it's virtues, but it also has its drawbacks. I think the biggest drawback here was that moment "A" stood for moment "A" and moment "B" stood for moment "B" and so on. You were *manipulating* the life rather than allowing the life to *emerge*.

The danger of knowing — consciously or subconsciously — why you're doing what you're doing, instead of forgetting why, is a big problem in acting. The two or three people I work very well with always come up to me and say: "Why do you think I am dumb? I'm very bright." And I have to go out of my way to say: "I don't think you're dumb, let's just suspend intelligence for a while in order to do the work differently. The less we both know about what we're doing, the better off we are."

For example, [*Yelena*], when you have a line that is interesting, you stop and you tell us that you *know* it's interesting. And by that time it loses its suddenness, it loses its — sense of jumping out and being — unprotected. It should just be unprotected and unfinished and then — on to the next moment! It's like the way people scratch their head or their knee or adjust their tie. The way people move their hands. It's — something! But it shouldn't be framed as an interesting moment. It just — is! It just exists without your comment on it, your knowledge that as an actor or director, you are pointing something out about the text.

There's another problem I think that you all should be watching, which is, you were making decisions about values in this material and you were making judgements about the material. I think I suggested before, and this is one of the Chekhov lines, that there is no judgement made on the material. What is interesting is the fact that the *life* appears, and then somehow, you say "Oh! that is what life is all about." Rather than making a plan: "This is what life is all about," and going on to show that.

Because of that, the scenes became a little too problematic, they became a little too definite, they became too much about "This is what I have to talk about" or "This is what I have to do" or "This is what I really want to say." For example, it stretches credibility that you, [*Serebrayakov*], would be such an awful person in the very beginning, that you would be so upset. I don't mean this as an interpretation about the character. It's just that once you somehow pass judgement on this character's problems, once you make this man totally impossible as a human being, then the problem has been articulated. When the problems have been articulated, the problems are no longer great. (*Nikos then proceeds to analyze and act out a portion of the scene.*) It's like:

As Serebrayakov: "Who's here, who's here Sonya —?"

As Yelena: (*Gently, lovingly:*) "No, darling, that's me."

As Serebrayakov: (*Eagerly, urgently:*) "Oh it's you, good, let me talk to you, let me talk to you."

(*Nikos acts out Yelena's inner world with expectation and eagerness.*) So, Yelena, you go closer to talk, you want to talk, but instead of him telling you about whatever is in his heart, he says:

As Serebrayakov: "You know, I have a problem, I have gout, my leg hurts." "You know what they say about Turgenev?" And so you go closer, you think you'll hear something exciting about Turgenev. That's one of the reasons you married him, because he says exciting things about Turgenev! And instead he says:

As Serebrayakov: (Flatly:) "Turgenev got angina because of gout." (*After the laughter, Nikos continues.*) So you see, it is not that these people's needs are different, it is that the world has changed for them. He is not an impossible person, he is in pain. It is the world, not the two of you, that breaks you apart.

The scene started with such a level of disgust on your part, [*Serebrayakov*], and on your part, [*Yelena*] at such a level of ignoring him. What is interesting about that? Ignoring him is not interesting, because you can get up and leave and go to a corner, you can go even further and leave the room. Ignoring someone on stage is never interesting. What is obviously interesting for you as an actress is to have to sit next to him, to have to listen to all of it, and say (*Gently:*) "Yes, dear, No, dear," — and not being able really to express your feelings. Same thing with you, [*Serebrayakov*]. You say things like (*Vulnerably, openly:*) "Listen, nobody's really paying any attention to me." But it's not interesting if you make it very clear, as you did now, that the things you say are not interesting. Then you *deserve* for people to not pay attention to you and the fact that she does not pay attention to you is nothing really new, but a kind of ordinary occurrence. And then we don't want to listen to you either, we dismiss you. What is interesting about a scene where a boring person is being ignored by someone?

You all had a tendency to come on stage only to deal with problems. You were very goal-directed toward the "problem" in the scene, rather saying to yourself: "There are no problems, I am are just really leading a life." Once you lead a life, then the problems develop. You were not taking the time in your acting to just lead your life.

For example, after this scene between Yelena and Serebrayakov, Sonya enters. You entered and went directly to them, as if to solve a problem. Instead, if you had gone around the room as you're talking, thinking "Now what should I do? Lights, we don't need lights, I'll blow out candles, I'll arrange something," then you would find that in the *middle* of this life, the other things come out. So it doesn't become about making pointed statements. You were making pointed statements in your acting about this or about that, rather than just saying (*As if with a shrug:*) "Well, that's what life is: I hate, I love, I want to do this, I want to do that, I sit, I pay attention, I don't pay attention."

Connect to other people on stage with you too; look at them; establish that it's not always a relationship between the person who talks to the person he's talking to, but to the life that is going on. Remember that in this material important things come out of unimportant things, and the important and the unimportant have equal weight. You were all, really, on such a suicidal level of existence! You had no life, you only had problems! You can't really do that, because you'd never make it to the third act, let alone the rest of your life! I mean, it has to be (*In an offhand, meandering way:*) "I talk, I talk about this, I talk about the world," and somebody says "Play the guitar." (*With surprise:*) "Ah! You ask me to play, I'll play." And someone else says: "Wait! I don't want to fight you now, I'm listening to the guitar." And someone else says: "So, oh well, I don't like the way you play the guitar, so let me tell you something." You know, if you go someplace and somebody makes a production number about playing the guitar, even if you have a problem, you suspend your problem for a little and you stop and listen to the guitar.

In essence, it's allowing the life to come in. Chekhov doesn't move from big crisis to big crisis. I mean, you were all so undone! I didn't think that you all could really survive another second up there. You were all suicidal, you were all hysterical, and it was not *life* that was creating your problems, *you* were creating your problems! Theoretically you should be perfectly normal, fun-loving people who care, who have relationships, who are just fine, except life creates problems for you. We begin to see that life has created certain problems because one of them has aged and one of them happens to be attractive, and one of them loves working but it gets too much for her, and one of them drinks.

Okay, Vanya's entrance. First of all, except for your words, I never knew that you have a world that you don't want to share with the other people, that makes you vulnerable. And then, all of a sudden, everyone but Yelena disappears and you start dealing with her from your secret world, (*Urgently, pressured:*) in a very important way, and you start talking to her and exposing yourself and becoming vulnerable to her and opening up. But your tone of talking to her was very similar to the way you talked to everyone else, only the words were different. Obviously, we talk one way to Sonya, one way to Yelena, to the nurse we talk a third way. Remember to deal with the adaptation, remember to shift the way that you talk to somebody, before the definite line, right? You don't have to wait for the line saying "I love you," before it's clear that you really love that particular character.

And then, Vanya, it would be great for you to let just loose, because all of sudden here's your chance. Remember how beautifully it's constructed. A lot of people, unimportant action, then suddenly you're all by yourself with only one person, *the* person, and you let loose and you don't know what to say! Find springboards to let loose, find ways that the material is so exciting to you, find things you want to do that are so exciting, that what you end up saying is never really calculated but just kind of pours out, and the words are far too few for all the things you have to say to her! Your acting was right on the money: very, very accurate, which is a similar problem, [*Sonya*], that you had in the last scene. Your words became measured rather than: "I have three thousand words to say, but I'm not selecting them, ten of them just surface accidentally without me knowing which ones."

Don't go up there and do something until at the end you say "Oh, boy, was that foolish!" You were never foolish enough and accidental enough with that scene [*between Vanya and Yelena*]. I don't know, I don't know if you should stutter, I don't know if you should trip over things, if you should try to sing to her. If it could just pour out, if it could have some sense of the privacy that creates foolishness, then I think the scene would've been more interesting for you.

There was something very moving with the monologue, [*Vanya*]. But you were only using the monologue to solve something on your mind, something you were preoccupied with. I just wish you would let loose and not keep score. Remember, you're alone on stage. If someone is alone on stage, then they can be foolish, right? I mean then they can just say, (*Eagerly, loosely:*) "Oh, God, to be free of imposition of having someone else around here (*Chaotically:*) and she says this, and she says that, and I wonder — (*Yelling, all-out:*) WHY!!!"

The playwright does not give you lines like: "Let me think about this, and let me think about that." He gives you a speech where you're frustrated because of something that you're not able to achieve. So, hit your head, sing it, pour the wine all over you, drink, stuff yourself with bread. Find things that allow a great deal of freedom for you rather then (*Pensively:*) "My mind is involved with the subject, I'm trying to solve it, I'm trying to figure it out." You were mesmerized with your problems. Use the text much more, as I keep saying, as a springboard rather than an imposition. It was too much of an imposition for you and it became thoughtful rather than open, and being about how when you're alone on stage you can do any kind of damn thing you want.

You know what it is, obviously? It's just much more interesting if we do not know *why* we are saying things. That's what I mean about not making judgements. Vanya, Astrov, in the next scene, between the two of you, you both were very alive on the stage, which was wonderful, but again, you were very problematic with things, you were too definite. Astrov comes in, and how much more exciting it would have been on your part if you did not *know* this was a conversation. Somebody brings you in to tell you something and you say (*Pouring out, carelessly:*) "Fine, fine, I don't know what to do, I mean, I do this, I do that…" Why? Because people allow themselves to open up when they are not pinned down. You see, if you assume that the other character will never really quote you or doesn't hold something against you, then the speeches will be more free for you. If you don't suspect that Vanya loves Yelena, then you can really go up to him, and basically say (*Openly:*) "She's a splendid woman. You know, isn't that interesting what people do? I mean why do they do that?" And the same thing with you, [*Yelena*], it's "Look sweetheart, look Sonya, I don't know why you're asking me questions but thank God you're asking me things." Then it becomes much more frightening for you. It is frightening because you're not in control of it.

Chekhov always gives you the wrong person opening up to the wrong person. I mean, you have Trofimov and Ranevskaya in *The Cherry Orchard;* Andrei in *The Three Sisters* talks at length to a man who can't hear, Ferapont. And the reason Chekhov does this is really very simple — so that you don't have to be careful. If the playwright is going to give you careless moments, moments where your soul comes out without manipulation, then you really have to allow yourself to part with information carelessly, freely.

How much more interesting if this conversation between Vanya and Astrov was really two interrupted monologues between the two of you. You don't know what he thinks, he doesn't know what you're thinking, so you can open up completely. I thought, [*Vanya*], it got kind of shy for you, it got all about one element of the character. Don't assume that character is something that's consistent on stage, especially in Chekhov. You could have been nasty, you could have been mean, you could have been temperamental, you could have been a lot of things if it all came out of the same kind of source. I thought that you found something wonderful but you hid behind it, you did not allow yourself to deal with all the other aspects that are also part of that whole strategy.

In the scene with Astrov and Sonya, Sonya says "Look I want to find out something, suppose I had a sister and she loved you, what would you do?" Instead of taking your time and reflecting on this, instead of guarding your response, suppose Astrov is just caught completely off guard! So he says (*Mildly panicked, as if thrown off and suddenly on the run:*) "Well, darling, I don't know what I would do, I really don't, I've got to go! Well, maybe I'd tell her this, I'd better go!" (*Upset:*) "How the hell do I know what I'd do? Well, bye, I'm out!"

What I'm saying is that then it becomes *life's* problem or *life's* virtue or *life's* glory, not *your* problem or *your* glory. Acting should obviously be in spite of yourself rather than because of yourself, and the best acting comes from finding and heightening those particular circumstances that allow you to be thrown off. I thought you [*Astrov*] played with definition, but you really played it as if you were aiming *directly for* this, and aiming *directly* for that, so it became functional rather than really caught by surprise.

Emily, I thought it was the best acting I've seen you do, really. But I wish you would get annoyed occasionally, I wish you would deal with some other elements of Sonya. For example, it could be (*With annoyance and frustration, Nikos says Sonya's line to Astrov, yelling it.*) "Come on, I beg you, don't drink!"

As Astrov: (*Quickly, contritely:*) "Okay, I won't drink, take the bottle."

As Sonya: (*Taken aback:*) "Oh."

As Astrov: (*Chastised:*) "Well, okay, I'll leave."

As Sonya: "Well, I mean, don't go. Have some cheese."

And then, Sonya, you are so happy that he stays, and you like to wait on him and make him happy, and all of a sudden you find yourself pouring the bottle and giving him a drink!

You are all laughing because that's exactly it. I wish you people were dealing more with the craziness and arbitrariness of life that comes naturally out of the circumstances and out of a certain kind of impact that you have on each other.

Now, the final scene between Sonya and Yelena. I thought that once again, Yelena, you did not let it come out. You were very careful in parting with your information, rather than playing the circumstances which are that the two of you have become friends. So that you spin around, so that the one keeps pouring wine for the other, et cetera. You kept making decisions before you were doing something. You did not have that sense of life going on. It was almost as if life existed only in your short sentences, and in between you were both moving away and becoming distant. I wish the drinking would continue, I wish the hugging would continue, I wish the crying would continue, I wish you would throw things at each other. There were too many decisions before the event. Things were taken too literally. Don't be so careful.

Find the life of the scene, which obviously here is two people becoming friends and opening up. It's one woman who is really not dealing with the "man" issue because she considers herself unattractive and another woman not dealing with the "man" issue because she is married. It's about these two women having a girl talk, you know what I mean? It's like a Thirties movie where the two women go to the ladies room and put lipstick on and exchange white furs! There is that kind of a madness to it and I wish you'd find that in the scene.

Put scenes on the right track without judgement. Put them on track in terms of the particular situations that actually exist, which are (*Carelessly, easily:*) two women all alone drinking and picking up plates and having some food and eating some of the cheese and cleaning up and lying down possibly, or going all over the stage, throwing things at each other. Why do you need that? You need these things in order to create continuity so that whatever lines you come out with don't become: "I am saying this to score a point, I am saying that to score a point." So that whatever scoring of points there is becomes accidental. It's just people who start talking, not knowing where they are going with it. Which is much more interesting than people who have a plan about how to score points and then speak. Yeah, Katherine?

ACTRESS: (*Playing Yelena:*) Okay, say we get to this point where we are friends and we trust each other —

NIKOS: Right.

ACTRESS: And we start talking and suddenly I realize — I love the doctor. Can I show that to her? How do I —

NIKOS: Well, I would say, if you suddenly make the realization that you love the doctor, what would you do?

ACTRESS: I would hide it.

NIKOS: How would you hide it? How would you do it? I mean, what do you think is the most interesting way of hiding it?

ACTRESS: Ignoring it.

NIKOS: Well, but you have a whole speech about him! You have all those lines about him, so you're not ignoring it! This is so-called script interpretation, dear, it's basic. Wait, wait. How can you make a choice to ignore it, to hide it? If the playwright gives you lines like (*Energetically:*) "No, no, no, the doctor, he plants trees, he does this, it's not the trees it's not the forest, it's — love! What does it matter if he drinks!" You're not hiding it if you say all these glorious things about what this man is. If the two of you exchange all those ideas, Yelena is not hiding it! Sonya asks you, "Are you happy?" And you say, "No." I mean, you do say (*Heartfelt:*) "No." Now! If you start calculating after she says "Are you happy?" if you think (*Measured:*) "Now wait, if I tell her I'm unhappy she'll assume it's the father, she'll assume it's Astrov," then you'll never be able to say the line that Chekhov has given you. The line that Chekhov has given you is (*Loudly, plaintively, honestly:*) "NO!" That line is the truth! So it just has to come out.

    The same with the line (*In a way so self-evident that it's funny:*) "Of course I wish I had married somebody else, but I didn't marry somebody else!" These things just kind of pour out. In the same way, it's just (*With abandon:*) "I feel, I feel, like playing the piano, that's what

I feel like doing, I feel like playing the piano!" And if you start doing things with your fingers, like cracking your knuckles (*The description rises to a crescendo:*) and you go to the piano and open the piano and fling the music up in the air, then your body will start to interpret for you. (*More and more an aria:*) And you hear the watchman making noise outside, and you yell at him, "Shut up! Get out of there! Don't knock! (*Long, drawn out, recklessly:*) "I'm PLAYING!!!! AHHHHH!"

(*The actress playing Yelena is in tears.*)

(*Softly:*) You see? Now you are crying. That's what the scene is all about. And then Sonya comes back in and says you can't play. If you've done all these things, then you are free to just *react*. But it's not like (*In a measured, calculated way:*) "Aha! I feel like playing the piano so I will because I want to demonstrate to you how good I feel." So that it becomes score one, score two, score three points.

Remember that between goals in any kind of game that you watch around, you know, this town! — there's a lot of playing. But you go up on stage and you refuse to carry the ball! You only want to score points! You know what I mean? That's exactly what it is, you only care for scoring, and therefore you lose the "game-ness" of it. Use that analogy in order to assume that what's interesting for you is playing. Because, really, it's the playwright who scores, not you. Chekhov takes you to the three moments or the five moments or the ten moments in each act where the points are scored. Any good playwright does that, and obviously he's a very good playwright. So be sure that you don't stop the life of the scene to make a judgement about the importance of the scene, or the importance of a specific moment. Then you will find out how exhilarating, how effortless it is to just play.

You know, [*Vanya*], if you just went into that monologue like (*With abandon:*) "What the hell," he gets down on the floor, he hits the floor, he lies on the table; then *they*, the audience, will interpret for you. They will say, "Aha! He feels this way or that way." Don't do the audience's work for them. They are there to make the interpretations, not you. You know what I mean? Everything you said had a purpose. People only do that in business, not on stage. When I go and try to raise money for the theater, I have to be very careful about the things I say. Because those guys don't want to listen to emotional things about the work, they want specifics. But if you're going to be up on that stage it has to be just the opposite. You have to deal with the whole life of it. The scene between the two of you [*Yelena and Sonya*] was so guarded that every statement was a cover for a cover for a cover rather than, "Boy, we have all these marvelous things to say to each other!"

I also think you should all be much more physical. Wouldn't it be wonderful if you fell on the floor and grabbed him, if the wine spilled and the candle dripped all over her? It's this kind of thing that would have given more immediacy and more life. What you really have to develop is a lack of reverence for each one of the lines, and a feeling that each one of the lines represents another twenty-six things that you have underneath. So that the lines become much more accidental.

You've got to trust the playwright. And if you trust the playwright you do not measure things, you're not careful with things. If you really trust the playwright, you assume that it is all going to happen without you doing it consciously. I remember the first time I did *Three Sisters* I found out that it was much better if I rehearsed all the scenes totally out of order. And the reason I continue to do that is just to get people to play little moments here and there, to just assume that there are all these little pieces of life that exist all on their own, and then eventually you put it all together. Each moment has to have some kind of interest and fascination but no judgement about what it means in the overall scheme of the play. Then it all comes out in a much more human way.

It's always wonderful if every time you do a Chekhov play if one of the actors is totally undisciplined. It's not that you want an undisciplined production, but it's interesting how electric something becomes with one person who is totally undisciplined. The first time I did *Three Sisters,* Olympia Dukakis who played Olga was such an undisciplined — wonderful actress — but undisciplined actress. So she'd just kind of move all over the stage and do all these things and everybody would have such a tough time! I mean in a good sense! Everybody would have such a tough time trying to find her! The same way with Austin Pendleton, he keeps thinking of different things all the time to do on the stage, intuitive and instinctive things, totally unrelated things. Blythe Danner's Nina — we never set that last scene. And every night I watched it and she let loose in a different way. She gave herself the freedom to move through that material in way that allowed all sorts of colors and textures to emerge — but almost unconsciously, you know? Chris Walken, too. I mean, Walken never knows at all what he does, or why he does it, or what he's going to do next. That's what makes him so riveting.

So don't try to score points. That's what I'm saying. Because when you keep score, you only count those big moments, you only judge certain moments important rather than the whole fabric. That's why, [*Vanya*], although you were alive, you were aiming directly for the kill, rather than saying (*Nonchalantly:*) "I don't know what's going on." Then you'd find out that all your crosses would've been much more interesting. I know you didn't rehearse it in this room, but, if you're going to come into a room, don't go directly for who you're going to talk to! Just come on in! (*Rambling, expansive:*) Come in, get behind the chair, look what is going on, and then realize, "Oh, God, I have to go to him," and then go to him. Don't open the door and immediately be ready to deliver the line. Come in for something else: Come in to pick up a book, come in to find a candle, and in between you say the line. The reason I'm saying that is so you're constantly active and alive, rather than only active and alive in the big important moments in the play. Because then you have no life. Then, really, you go from head-step to head-step and you don't ever climb the staircase.

Don't sacrifice the process to deal with the obvious results that are pointed up in the play. I've said many times that in Chekhov, getting there is *all* the fun. Not *half* of the fun, not *most* of the fun. Getting there is *all* the fun.

COMMENTARY
BY AUSTIN PENDLETON

Austin Pendleton began his career and has acted and directed many times at the Williamstown Theatre Festival. He has appeared in the first New York productions of Oh Dad, Poor Dad..., Fiddler on the Roof, The Sorrows of Frederick, *and* Doubles, *among others. He is a playwright (*Booth *and* Uncle Bob*), director (*Spoils of War, The Runner Stumbles *and* Elizabeth Taylor in The Little Foxes*), teacher (HB Studio), and member of Chicago's Steppenwolf Ensemble. His film credits include* What's Up Doc?, Trial and

Error, The Mirror Has Two Faces, Mr. and Mrs. Bridge, Catch-22, *and* Amistad, *and has also worked extensively on television.*

Reading this wonderful book, this invaluable book, has been a dizzying, exhilarating, disorienting, transcendent, and troubling experience. It has been in other words, like working with and around Nikos. It has made it hard for me to write about knowing Nikos in any large, generalized sense. It has reduced me to anecdote.

I met Nikos in the spring of 1957, when my cousin Lila and I (a college freshman and a high-school senior, respectively) traveled from our hometown in Ohio to New York on our spring breaks to audition for the apprentice program at what was then called, with already uncalled-for modesty, the Williamstown Summer Theatre. The auditions were held at the Williams Club on East 39th Street and Nikos conducted them; this was to be the Theatre's third season but its first as an Equity company and its first with an apprentice program.

Lila and I presented the great fight scene between Amanda and Tom in *The Glass Menagerie.* This scene climaxes with a long speech by Tom, a diatribe against Amanda, which I began on a high pitch with a voice that even now, forty-one years later, some people are unkind enough to suggest has a tendency toward shrillness — and was at that time unmodulated by all the patient, brilliant voice teachers who have since labored away at it. I must have been about halfway through the speech, plowing through it in the face of Nikos' visible agitation, when he stopped me, and, clearly distressed at the crushing blow he had dealt to what he must have known were weeks of preparation and years of aspiration, said "I know the speech can go higher," conveying with these words a doleful sense of the abyss that would be revealed were I to climb on toward these heights.

We were dismissed very politely and got back in the car to drive the eight hours back to Ohio. Two months later we learned that we had been accepted into the program.

We learned this days before the company was to assemble, and when we got to Williamstown we found there were only eleven apprentices (in certain subsequent summers there have been about a hundred). Undaunted by these clear signs of the desperation with which we had been chosen, I spent the summer trying very hard to get a leading role in one of the productions. When not ineptly helping to build the sets, I would insist on auditioning for such roles as (I confess it) Rodolpho in *A View from the Bridge*. Nikos was known as an impatient man, but he sat through these auditions with a fortitude that makes me think now he must have been atoning for some ancient, ineradicable sin. And it was with the most tortured, compassionate obliqueness that he would communicate to me that none of these parts were to be mine.

Why did he do this? I wondered about it even then. I'd like to say that some talent was visible beneath these desperate attempts of mine, but I'm pretty sure this was not so. The answer may lie in this book. Because in this book you read the words of, and can virtually hear, a brilliant man clawing again and again through the rubble of defensiveness, evasion, and simple lack of craft, trying to get to a heartbeat he is pretty sure — or maybe simple hopes — that he has heard. To this end he employs a really funny wit, and awesome gift for what I think the French call *tirade*, an eager patience sometimes, a violent lack of patience other times, and best of all an astonishing set of insights into the material being performed (this final section of the book contains the most exciting revelation of what an actor must locate in the plays of Shaw that I have ever read, and I think the same goes for what he says about how to work on Chekhov).

Nikos was a wonderful director, sometimes a great one, and like all great ones, sometimes awesomely wrong-headed. His best work is some of the best I've ever seen or had the privilege to act in. He was a profound teacher, profound in his search, profound in his effect, profound in his sense of the terrifying process that learning how to act is and has to be. Learning from him (and this occurred in rehearsals, of course, as well as in the classroom) was like being picked up from a beach (on which you might have been having a perfectly satisfactory picnic, thank you very much) by a giant tidal wave and carried far, far inland, often to be deposited on a mountaintop with a view of things that you have never dreamed of. I'm glad this book exists. It captures him — well no, it doesn't capture him (he was a tidal wave, remember?). But it evokes him. I can't imagine anyone reading this book and saying, "Well, I guess you had to be there." Read this book and you are there, and better for it.

Afterword
Come to the Edge
BY TOM MOORE

In the theater, Tom Moore is best known as the director of 'night, Mother *(which won the Pulitzer Prize and for which he received his second Tony nomination), and the original* Grease, *one of the longest-running shows in the history of Broadway. Other Broadway productions include* Moon Over Buffalo, Once in a Lifetime, Division Street, *and* The Octette Bridge Club. *He has worked at Mark Taper Forum, ACT, Guthrie and Arena Stages, the Old Globe, and WTF. He directed the film of* 'night, Mother *and episodes of* ER, Mad About You, *(with Emmy nominations for both)* Cheers, Picket Fences, Civil Wars, *and* Northern Exposure. *He has taught and directed at SUNY Buffalo, Brandeis, and the University of London, England. He is featured in the Pennebaker/Hedges documentary* Moon Over Broadway.

The following is edited from a two-hour conversation Tom and I had at a restaurant in Los Angeles.

Nikos played a very large part in my development as a director, and his influence on my past, present, and future professional life is enormous. He was without question the most important directing teacher I've ever had, and his encouragment at the embryonic start of my career was inestimable. You know what I miss most? Nikos believed in me. As a student, and later as a collaborator. Almost every summer, I would get that telephone call from him inviting me back to Williamstown. And although I didn't always go back, it meant a lot that I could always count on hearing from him. I think it's a healthy response to want to have mentors in our lives. I tend to turn myself over to certain people I trust, and in losing Nikos I miss that trust. Of course, we had a mutually healthy use for each other; I know that I used Nikos for what he taught me and I also knew that as I became commercially successful, he used that for his theater. But the point is, he had the ultimate confidence in me and he proved it by asking me to be there long before I had commercial success, and that makes a big difference. I mean, once you hit a certain point, who cares if they want you! That's nice, but it's like: Why wouldn't they?

You can't ever replace the people in your life you grew up with — because they are the people who know you in a way no one else can. In this case I didn't grow up *with* but grew up *under,* but it's still the same thing. I developed as a director under Nikos. You know, as I sit here talking to you — and I'm particularly very aware of this with people dying all around us now — but I hope Nikos knew how great his influence on us was. When I started out as a director, I tended to be safe in all things. I wasn't about to throw something up on the stage until I had confidence in it. And somehow that confidence was built through Nikos. Simply by having him point out what was good and what was bad. It was specific. You know, so much of what we are taught, and later the criticism we are given, is not specific. It isn't very usable. I had some intelligent, often very talented people teach me, but I really didn't learn anything about directing. I got some encouragement, I learned something about the literature of the piece, but with Nikos you actually found out something about directing. The miracle of Nikos was his ability to see a scene through *your* eyes. I mean, I can critique a scene, but to critique it means directing it. Nikos had the gift of being able to say, "Well, you seem to be aiming for such and such here, and this is where you failed." And most people can't do that. They see it through how *they* would do it. And that really wasn't what he did. He critiqued through *your* objectives. I haven't met anyone else who's done that. I was thinking about Yale as I drove here, I saw the whole lineup of all of us sitting in that front row of his Drama 10 class at Yale — in the experimental theater — it is indelibly etched in my mind. And each of us had very different styles. And I don't recall him ever attempting to make any of us in any kind of mold.

I think all of us in the arts seek a way of developing some sort of aesthetic. And I think the aesthetic is a combination and a substance of who you get influenced by. Until I read some of these critiques, I'd forgotten just how rich Nikos' grasp of the material was. What a breadth of knowledge he had of theater and literature! It often irritates me that people think they can do anything — directors or actors — without a certain knowledge of the material, genre, and history of the play and its place in the literature. What's fascinating to me throughout the book is Nikos' very different ways of approaching different writers. For example, what he says about Shaw — it's similar to how I feel about directing Shakespeare. If you do not know how to speak the iambic pentameter,

I don't care what the hell you have as an idea or concept. And Nikos is saying Shaw's the same. And Brecht. And Chekhov. If you don't go by their rules, if you don't know the rules inherent to each of these playwrights, it really doesn't matter what else you bring to it. I think this material should be very provocative for people. I mean, Nikos is setting up a very definite idea here. That chapter on Shaw — if you come away from that with nothing except that Shaw is about playing a positive against a positive, you have a formidable tool to use. A very specific tool. I mean, I've never gotten Shaw. I like to watch Shaw, but I've never gotten it. It's ideas rather than emotion, and I don't respond to that. But here's a way to look at Shaw! And it never would've crossed my mind! It's fascinating. You see that when Nikos makes a critique it's not just based on a idea, but a breadth of knowledge. A considered opinion, a meeting of the intellectual with the theatrical, which I just don't think happens very often.

I remember a lot of Nikos phrases — "plastic values" was one of my favorites, because nobody uses that. By that he meant the theatrical stuff you add to a play, whether it be music or sound, or scenic elements. That made a big impression on me because those elements are what first attracted me to the theater. I was very much influenced by a director I worked with in college, Joe Stockdale, and by another wonderful teacher at Yale, Gordon Rogoff. But Nikos defined it, delineated it. I could quarrel with some of Nikos' directing — (the Chekhovs excepted because his Chekhovs were always amazing). But I don't think there has ever been an American scene critic like Nikos.

When I first studied with Nikos in 1965, I was terrified. First of all, he was legendary at that point. Without question, he was *it*. Basically, his Drama 10 course was the essence of your education at

Yale. I have very few strong memories of that first year except Nikos. To prove yourself to him was your goal pure and simple. And when I got to Yale I didn't really know what I was doing. I'd directed one ten-minute play in college. I'd been a political science major, and switched over to speech and drama in my junior year. So that whole first semester I felt like I was just waiting to be found out.

Oh, Nikos knew what he was doing in terms of intimidation! I mean, you knew exactly where you stood. It was awesome because he would stand there when a scene was happening and he would have his note cards, and on that note card you could see him write a number and circle it. And the lower your number, the lower your spirits fell. And you would also be seated from the best director on down. Now maybe this is my memory. Maybe this was my fear! But that's the way I tend to recall it. The directors would sit in the first row, and the first and second year actors behind you, so it was a big crowd.

I don't think Nikos took me seriously the whole first semester. You never knew what he thought, but I don't believe he ever focused on me. At that point the star of the class was a brilliant guy named Larry Madison — by far the best director in our group. You'd sit back and just be in awe. And clearly, Nikos thought his work was impressive too. And then there was an intellectual director named Ted Cornell who I knew was a Nikos favorite, but whose work was very opposite Nikos' style. Then there was Jeff Bleckner who switched over from acting. Richard Place, who was very into antiwar plays, Sandy Manley who became a press agent, and Charles Dillingham who became a managing director, and several others. Anyway, we had come to the end of the first semester — we each had directed a lot of scenes. And we had to put on a major project. I did a piece from *The Ballad of the Sad Cafe*. Jeff

Bleckner and David Clennon and Joan Pape were in it. I condensed it, and it was highly theatrical, and presentational. And lo and behold, it was a great success. Something had happened to me that semester. I was braver, and more confident. I had begun to develop an aesthetic, a style. And I will never forget this! Looking at Nikos' face as we always did, with hope and anticipation of judgement. But as I looked at his face this time, I realized that something was now very different. It was a miracle. I had wanted his approval so badly and had never gotten it, and then finally, there it was — focus. On me for the first time. And when he critiqued the piece he gave us full credit for everything we had done, and particularly for the boldness of the endeavor. That was the turning point. From then on, I was a real director.

To get Nikos to like you was a horrifying prospect because you felt that if you didn't, you had failed totally. I remember so many things about individual scenes. Maybe it was because the desperation was so high, trying to figure out what to do! There's a certain narcissism which I think is in all of our lives, but there's a particular narcissism in my memory! It was as if nobody else existed, because I was trying so hard to stay afloat. So I only saw everyone else as competitors. And that's certainly something Nikos encouraged, which some people might say was a negative. And it did seem gratuitously cruel sometimes. When Nikos talked, it was so short. It was not padded. He didn't have much patience. I don't think of Nikos as being necessarily a kind person. He was certainly kind to me and extremely generous to me, but if he didn't feel that someone was of interest to him, he didn't necessarily go out of his way to help them.

At the same time he could be very nurturing. He would protect you, too. I remember once we had an assignment to do a comic scene and I knew *Auntie Mame* because I had seen it in college, so I did a scene from that. And I remember one of the directors — I won't mention the name — who said, "I don't think that's worthy to be doing here." And Nikos came down on him quickly and resolutely, and said, "Don't be such a snob, this is part of our theatrical heritage. The problems of staging this material are worth figuring out." There's a lot of nonsense that goes on in any kind of class, in any kind of theatrics, people talking a lot of bullshit, and he really didn't have much time for that — you always felt he was on the run, on the verge of catching the next train out that afternoon! (Which was usually the case.) So what he had to say was precise and to the point. Being scared of where you ranked created such a tension, but I think that's what you needed to survive in his class and not buckle, and I think it prepared us well for the professional theatre that lay ahead.

Nikos couldn't or wouldn't be consistent. Which is much like directing often goes. You're not particularly consistent, you go with whichever way you think will speak to the problem. Nikos never thought consistency was a virtue anyway. He went on instinct, and ultimately that's what's going to make a distinction. When I first started doing film and television, I planned everything out in advance, because I didn't trust my instincts — the film of *'night, Mother* was planned out on a computer! But as I gained experience with cameras by doing a lot of television, I finally learned instinctively where to place the camera. It took a long time to get there. But in the end, it's trusting your instinct. If you have talent, I think that's the main thing a great teacher imparts to you. To inspire you, to challenge you, and then ultimately get you to trust whatever you bring to the table. Because if you don't, you're simply a copy of someone else.

The talent to teach is not the talent to direct. I'm not a very good teacher. Very few people can do both. What we may underestimate is Nikos' energy — and transferring that energy into people learning. There can be a passivity about directing and teaching, and there was nothing like that with Nikos. There was an excitement, the adrenalin always flowed, you never got bored. And maybe that's the ultimate thing all of us try to do in the theater anyway. If you can keep them from being bored, you've probably done two-thirds of your job. He cared. And I never felt he lost that passion. In Tyrone Guthrie's biography, he talks about one of a director's major jobs is keeping actors interested during rehearsal. Something like this: "If you can't keep actors interested during your rehearsal process, you should just fuckingly well keep out of the theater." I think that applies to Nikos too.

If Nikos liked you, he brought you into Williamstown; he kept that chain going. Only two years out of Yale — which impressed me — he offered me *Mother Courage*. When I got there to have my first meeting, Nikos and John Conklin and Santo LoQuasto who were designing the show had basically already worked out the entire concept. And I said: This is great, but it's not the way I see this. And I bring this up because for most people with a relatively green director, that could've been a deal-breaker for the rest of my life. But when I said I couldn't go in that direction, Nikos accepted it. With someone else, that might have led to a parting of the ways. But, as I said, every summer he would call.

There's something else I remember often, because now I'm constantly working with stars and I'm often up against a casting choice that's not what I think it should be. In 1979 I directed *Hay Fever* with Celeste Holm. I love Celeste and think she's a wonderful, talented actress.

But Celeste Holm is not the usual Judith. The usual Judith is big, more like Colleen Dewhurst, or Maggie Smith — a big voice. It's a part based on charm and bullying your way through the situation. And Celeste brought enormous charm and a delicacy to it. And I got frustrated because I had an idea about what it was supposed to be. And I went to Nikos, pulling my hair out, and said "Nikos, Nikos, I don't know what to do, this is not working, it's a mistake, what are we going to do?" But Nikos said a wonderful line to me — I think maybe he even wrote it to me, he said: "Tom, remember, sometimes it's better to anthologize the collection than to write the poem." And I knew exactly what he meant! It was like, relax, take the pieces that you're getting and put it together.

And that's what I do more now as a director than I ever did. I'm not really very interested in a "concept." I mean, I always have a concept, but I like to take what I get — if I cast well — and then edit. I love that about film. This is what you got, make it into something. Isn't that the hardest thing? Accepting limitations…and yet making them work for you?

One of the highlights of my time at WTF, a special memory, is *Our Town* with Geraldine Fitzgerald playing the Stage Manager — Nikos' idea. This was one of the best experiences of my life in theater. I can remember us out on that big, sweeping lawn, rehearsing the monologues, the clouds rolled by and Geraldine Fitzgerald walking the hills with her long gray hair flying, proclaiming those lines — "Twenty years from now, a hundred years from now —" that speech about what life will be like in the future. And the real stage manager and myself were in tears. And I remember vividly the rehearsal we held of Act II in the Williamstown cemetery, as the entire cast trouped through the gravestones with their umbrellas on a hot summer day.

Nikos gave you complete freedom. I mean, he would come in, of course, and see the run-throughs and he'd give notes and share ideas. And even if you did sometimes feel the same terror and dread in the pit of your stomach just like you did in school, there was never a sense of — also just like in school — of him trying to shape it into something that was his. I think he took an enormous pride in people taking off on their own. There's a wonderful little poem — I'll paraphrase it now — but it reminds me of Nikos as a teacher.

Come to the edge —
I can't — I'll fall.
Come to the edge
— it's too far.
Come to the edge —
and I did, and he pushed me and I flew.

As he did with so many he influenced in his teaching, his directing, and his leadership of a theatre, he pushed us and we flew.

Nikos Psacharopoulos was born in Athens, Greece, and came to the United States at age seventeen. He received a BA from Oberlin College and an MFA from Yale School of Drama.

In 1955, he helped establish the Williamstown Theatre Festival and served as its Artistic/Executive Director from 1956 until his death in 1989. He directed ninety of the 223 Main Stage productions during his tenure there, including *Peer Gynt, Cyrano de Bergerac,* numerous versions of Chekhov including *The Three Sisters* and *The Sea Gull* (latter for PBS), *The Greeks* (U.S. premiere), *Trelawny of the 'Wells,' Undiscovered Country, Idiot's Delight,* the two-part, six-hour *Tennessee Williams: A Celebration,* and his last WTF production, the epic *Legend of Oedipus* conceived for WTF by Kenneth Cavander. Nikos also directed many Tennessee Williams plays including *The Glass Menagerie,* which moved to Long Wharf Theater and was the basis of a film version directed by Paul Newman. In the year before he died, Nikos staged *A Streetcar Named Desire* with Blythe Danner for Circle-in-the-Square on Broadway and *Sweet Bird of Youth* with Joanne Woodward at the Royal Alexandria Theatre in Toronto.

At WTF, Nikos worked with some of America's leading actors, directors, and designers, among them Karen Allen, Jeff Bleckner, Arvin Brown, Kate Burton, Richard Chamberlain, Stockard Channing, Stephen Collins, John Conklin, Tim Daly, Blythe Danner, Colleen Dewhurst, Richard Dreyfuss, Olympia Dukakis, Mildred Dunnock, Peter Evans, Geraldine Fitzgerald, Lee Grant, William Hansen, Rosemary Harris, Edward Herrmann, Peter Hunt, Stacy Keach, Frank Langella, Santo Loquasto, E.G. Marshall, Roberta Maxwell, Lynne Meadow, Tom Moore, Joe Morton, James Naughton, Carrie Nye, Austin Pendleton, Ellis Rabb, Christopher Reeve, Ann Reinking, Richard Thomas, Maria Tucci, Christopher Walken, Sigourney Weaver, Dianne Wiest, and Joanne Woodward.

Nikos also directed for American Shakespeare Festival, Pasadena Playhouse, New York City Opera (the U.S. and world premieres of *Lizzie Borden, Washington Square,* and *Miss Julie*), the New York Pro Musica (original staging for *The Play of Daniel* and *The Play of Herod,* performed at the John F. Kennedy Center, Westminster Abbey, and Italy's Spoleto Festival). He also directed Langston Hughes' *Tambourines to Glory,* one of the first black musicals on Broadway.

Nikos taught at Yale from 1956 to 1988 and was Visiting Professor/Lecturer at Williams, Columbia, NYU, and Amherst. He received honorary degrees from Siena and Emerson and was named a Doctor of Humane Letters at Williams. Nikos lived in New York City, Williamstown, New Haven, and on the Aegean island of Siphnos.

ACKNOWLEDGMENTS

Gregory Boyd, Steve Lawson, Lynne Meadow, Bonnie Monte, Tom Moore, Austin Pendleton, David Schweizer, and Joanne Woodward provide the narrative for *Toward Mastery* and I am enormously grateful to them for capturing Nikos' essence in such insightful, incisive, irreverent, and loving words.

My sister Joyce Hackett gave me the benefit of her expertise as a writer and editor; my sister Julie and her husband Alan Behr provided technical assistance and thoughtful suggestions. My friend Jessica Hecht (whose mastery in her craft as an actress is a privilege to watch) thoroughly read the manuscript in its initial stages, helping me with emphasis and clarity.

My agent Susan Schulman and my publishers Marisa Smith and Eric Kraus continue to be unwavering in their encouragement and support in expanding my vision and confidence as a writer.

Words are not adequate to express the extent of my gratitude to Steve Lawson, who patiently and generously read and re-read my manuscript; advising, editing, suggesting and collaborating with me every step of the way. His wit, his craft, his art are most obviously present in his words at the beginning of this book, but contribute as well to every page that follows. Steve often described working on this project as "a labor of love," and it was very moving for me to see in his efforts the reflection of his enormous love and regard for Nikos. For this I thank him most.

Finally, I would like to dedicate this book to my class at NYU — and to all those Nikos taught and worked with who still carry him with them in their hearts.

Jean Hackett graduated from NYU and studied acting at Circle-in-the-Square Theater School and the Royal Academy of Dramatic Art in London. While completing her training, she spent four seasons as a member of the Williamstown Theatre Festival's non-Equity company, and returned over the years as a member of the Equity company for several productions including Nikos' last, *The Legend of Oedipus.* Along with Steve Lawson and Nikos, she was co-adaptor of *Tennessee Williams: A Celebration,* a six-hour collage of scenes form all of Williams' plays with a cast of forty. Ms. Hackett has played roles on- and off-Broadway, at many of the country's leading regional theaters, and in television and film. She is the author of *The Actor's Chekhov,* which chronicles Nikos' work on the plays of Anton Chekhov.